31-12-2013.

Happy Birthday Ann.
with love from
Glenn, laura,
Matilda + Dot xxx

# Creative
# PAPER CUTTING

FIFTEEN PAPER SCULPTURES
TO INSPIRE AND DELIGHT

# Creative

## FIFTEEN PAPER SCULPTURES
## TO INSPIRE AND DELIGHT

# PAPER CUTTING

CHEONG-AH HWANG

THE GUILD OF MASTER CRAFTSMAN PUBLICATIONS

First published 2013 by
Guild of Master Craftsman Publications Ltd
Castle Place, 166 High Street, Lewes,
East Sussex BN7 1XU

Text © Cheong-ah Hwang, 2013
Copyright in the Work © GMC Publications Ltd, 2013

ISBN 978 1 86108 920 5

**Publisher** Jonathan Bailey
**Production Manager** Jim Bulley
**Managing Editor** Gerrie Purcell
**Senior Project Editors** Dominique Page, Sara Harper, Cath Senker
**Editor** Nicola Hodgson
**Managing Art Editor** Gilda Pacitti
**Designer** Simon Goggin

Set in Interstate
Colour origination by GMC Reprographics
Printed and bound in China

# Contents

# Introduction

This book shows you how to make bas-relief (low-relief) paper sculptures. A coin is a perfect example of a low-relief object; an image is slightly projected from its surface, showing only one side of its form. It is perceived by the shadows and reflections of light on its irregular surface. In paper sculptures, we achieve the same effect by cutting and pasting pieces of paper to a flat surface, often altering the surface of the cut paper to create a greater three-dimensional illusion.

When I was growing up, I remember seeing magazine advertisements that featured paper sculptures. But it wasn't until I was in my late 20s that I realized these pretty paper pictures were part of a discrete art form that used specific techniques and structures. I instantly felt that I had found the perfect vehicle for my creativity, and sought to learn more about paper sculpture from books and the Internet.

What so attracted me to paper sculpture is the illusion of depth. Even a paper sculpture that is only 1in (2.5cm) deep can create an illusion of the actual depth of the depicted object and its surroundings. Playing on the tension between two- and three-dimensional elements is enormous fun. It is exciting to witness the process of the paper pieces being shaped and put together, so that the sculpture not only depicts an image but also becomes an entity of its own. Another reason why I love paper sculpture is that, quite simply, I love paper. Paper is very easy to acquire and is extremely versatile: it cuts, curls, tears, stretches and creases with ease, and it retains its altered form. These characteristics enable us to mimic a variety of materials, such as stones, feathers or flower petals. I love the idea of using a plain, everyday material and turning it into something extraordinary.

Paper sculpture can make an excellent group activity because there are many stages to the process. You can gather a few family members or friends, assign a role to each person, and work together. It's a lot of fun, and makes the process quicker too. One person may be good at separating layers, while another may enjoy sculpting; one person can shape one layer, while another can shape a different layer.

I cannot emphasize enough the importance of recycling. Please try to use recycled paper, or recycled paper products, in your sculpture as much as possible. After you have finished your sculpture, sort the paper scraps and take them to the recycling centre.

I hope this book inspires you to explore your creativity and helps you at every step along the way.

**Cheong-ah Hwang**

# Materials

Part of the appeal of paper craft is that the materials are readily available. Most are easy to source, and you may already have some at home. It is possible to find substitutes for many items, so you will always have options. It is a good idea to check that your materials are available in the colours and sizes you want before starting your paper sculpture.

## Papers

As a professional, I need to consider the quality of the paper and its longevity. If these factors are important to you, look for terms such as 'acid-free', 'lignin-free', 'archival', 'pH-neutral' and 'buffered'.

Although high-quality paper lasts longer and cuts better, plain cardstocks or poster boards, available from craft stores, will work just fine to make gifts, cards and decor for your home.

I also strongly recommend that you recycle or upcycle everyday paper. There are so many paper products around us: copy paper, cupcake wrappers, paper plates, train timetables, cardboard boxes, gift wrap, paint card samples... Think about what you can do with them before throwing them out. Practise different techniques on them, or use them as fun accents on greeting cards or wall decor.

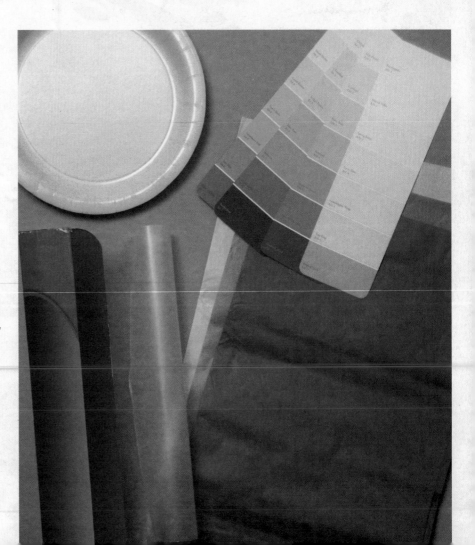

Have a range of paper and card to hand for your projects – always use recycled paper when you can.

# Different weights of paper

When choosing paper for sculpture, you need to think about how heavy the paper should be for the job. When there is a mystery paper with no gsm given, I use my own rough 'weighing' system: I hold the mid-point of the shorter edge of a sheet of 8½ x 11in (21.6 x 28cm), or A4, paper, then let it fall to one side. If the tip of the paper falls lower than my hand (image 1), it is lightweight (under 120gsm). If it falls around level with my hand (image 2) or parallel to the floor (image 3) the paper is medium-weight (120–200gsm). If the tip of the paper points upwards (image 4), it is heavyweight (above 200gsm).

Lightweight paper is thinner and more transparent than heavier papers. It is best to use lightweight paper for layering without supports, because the supports beneath can show through. Lightweight paper is good for making intricate cuts, crumpling and curling, but wrinkles very easily. You will need to use very little glue, or use adhesives that contain less moisture.

Medium-weight paper is good for all kinds of paper sculpting techniques and holds shapes very well. It is also opaque enough to use for layering with supports (see page 34). It can take glue better than lightweight paper.

Heavyweight paper adds dimension to a sculpture without supports or shaping. Note that it is much easier to achieve intricate cuts if good-quality heavyweight paper is used, but embossing, curling and crumpling will prove labour-intensive.

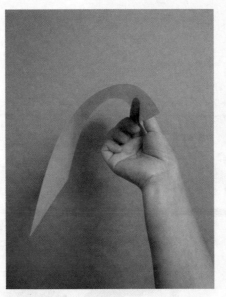

Lightweight (under 120gsm)

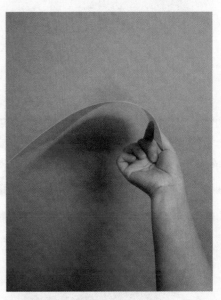

Medium-weight (120gsm)

Medium-weight (200gsm)

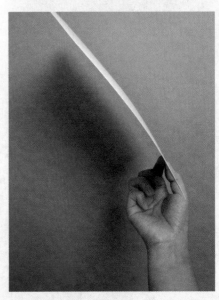

Heavyweight (over 200gsm)

# Types of paper

Described below are some of the papers that are most commonly used for paper sculpture. They are available in most art supply and craft stores.

### TRACING PAPER

Tracing paper is a versatile material: its translucency allows you to separate layers from a master template and to transfer a pattern onto another piece of paper. Plain lightweight tracing paper (40gsm) is sufficient for the job. You can also use it for sculpting. Use the paper as it comes for its soft translucency or crumple it to achieve crisp textures.

Tracing paper comes in pads, sheets or rolls. The projects in this book can be made using a 9 x 12in (23 x 30cm) or A4 sized pad. If you want to try a larger project, I recommend buying it on a roll.

### TISSUE PAPER

Tissue paper is even thinner than tracing paper and also translucent. It can be used for making delicate objects such as insect legs, antennae and flower petals. Apply glue to a small piece of tissue paper, twist it so it is hair-thin, then let it dry. By doing this, it will become more manageable and hold the shape better.

### VELLUM PAPER

One of my favourites, this is another translucent paper. Heavier than plain tracing paper; it is neither too clear nor too opaque. Its translucency adds an air of mystery to a sculpture. If you float it in front of a dark or colourful background it gives an illusion of depth of field.

Lightweight papers from top to bottom: tracing paper, tissue paper, vellum, unryu, Japanese paper.

Art papers: the top two sheets are watercolour papers; the bottom two sheets are printmaking papers.

Vellum is sold under many names: you may see it labelled as parchment paper, transparent paper, vellum paper, vellum, tracing paper, papier calque or embossing paper. It's best to look at it in person before buying rather than trying to order it online, unless the company has a good returns policy.

The vellum paper used for the projects in this book is made of cotton and weighs 90gsm. It varies in size. If you plan to work on a bigger project, check the size availability. There is also vellum available made from chemically treated paper, which gives the same effect as cotton vellum. It usually comes in small sizes in a variety of colours, and is easily found in craft stores. If you want to experiment with translucent effects, you could also try baking parchment, wax paper or glassine paper.

### JAPANESE PAPERS

These papers are lightweight, but very durable, and are used to create contrast and texture. There are many different kinds, some of which are handmade from plant fibres. Tearing the paper creates soft and fuzzy edges; the longer the fibres, the fuzzier the effect. Unryu paper in particular has very long, dense fibres. Use unryu paper to make animal fur or fuzzy plants.

### ART PAPERS

Watercolour and printmaking papers are long-lasting. They are medium- to heavyweight and can be expensive, but are very good quality. They are made of 100% cotton, and cut much better than wood-pulp paper. Even heavy watercolour paper allows very intricate patterns to be cut easily and cleanly.

Coloured drawing papers: their cotton content and weight make them ideal for paper sculpture.

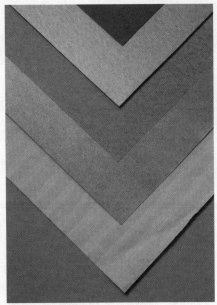

Cardstocks: these are less good for paper sculptures but are ideal for experimentation.

Foam and mat board: the top two sheets are examples of foam board; the bottom two are mat board.

## COLOURED DRAWING PAPERS

Also called charcoal or pastel papers, these papers come in deep and vibrant colours. They are used for pastel drawings, so the paper has a subtle texture on one or both sides. They have some cotton content, so they cut well. These papers have a good weight to them without being too heavy; embossing is easier and they hold shape well. All these factors make these papers among the best to use for paper sculpture.

## CARDSTOCKS

These papers come in the standard 8½ x 11in (21.6 x 28cm), or A4 size, which is a convenient size for small projects. Many of them are acid-free and come in a rich array of colours, patterns and textures, with weights ranging from light to heavy. Many cardstocks are made of recycled paper. They have no cotton (rag) content and are not the best for paper sculptures; however, they are good enough to use to have fun and explore your creativity.

## MAT BOARD

Most mat boards come in about 1/16in (1.5mm) thickness, or 4ply, so are very rigid. There are many different colours available. Mat board is used for backing your artwork.

## FOAM BOARD

Foam board has a soft core inside. It usually comes in a thickness of 3/16in (5mm), but is very lightweight. It is easy to cut and can be used for making supports for your sculptures or as a base when embossing paper. The surface can get damaged easily, so you need plenty of foam board to hand when embossing.

# Adhesives

When you make a paper sculpture, the layers need to be attached to each other (see page 35). There are many kinds of adhesive available, so make sure you know which one will be right for the job. I recommend using high-quality acid-free adhesives; poorer-quality ones may result in your sculpture falling apart, and may also cause the paper to deteriorate quickly.

## GLUE

I recommend using pH-neutral PVA (polyvinyl acetate) glue for longevity. It is white when wet but dries clear. It is also water-soluble, so, if necessary, it can be dissolved and removed so that the paper can be detached or repositioned. Use it sparingly – just a little dab of PVA glue can do a big job. Drop some glue on a glue reservoir (you could use the lid of an old jam jar), and use a pointed object such as an awl as a glue applicator. When gluing larger areas, drop some glue on the area, and spread it out thinly. You can also use this glue to strengthen a fragile piece of paper.

## PASTES

These are long-lasting and contain less moisture than glue, so are particularly useful for gluing lightweight paper. Paste takes longer to dry than glue does, so you will have time to reposition the paper if necessary. Like PVA, paste can be dissolved and removed if necessary. You can also dilute it, which makes it useful for applying thin glue to large areas. Paste is very sticky, and can be messy to work with.

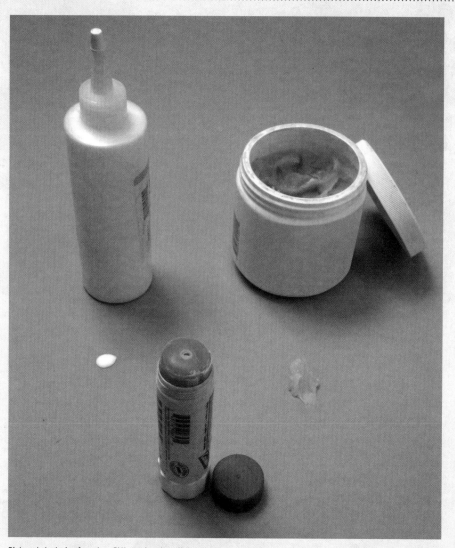

Pictured clockwise from top: PVA, paste, glue stick

## GLUE STICKS

Some glue sticks work well, but others don't, so you may need to try out a few to see what works best. They are convenient and less messy than other types of adhesive. However, so-called permanent glue sticks are often not permanent in practice, so make sure you apply the glue generously. Repositionable glue sticks are handy when you only need temporary assembly for your paper sculpture.

## MASKING TAPE

Masking tape (also known as painter's tape) is mostly used when painting and decorating; it protects areas that you don't want to be painted over. It tears easily and is less tacky than permanent tape. Masking tape is used in paper sculpture for securing cutting templates on paper. You can also use it for mounting paper sculptures to walls; it is strong enough to hold the paper, but does not damage the wall when it is removed. Masking tape comes in many sizes and colours. Acid-free tape is available from art supply stores, while the standard type can be bought from hardware stores.

## DOUBLE-SIDED ADHESIVE

Double-sided adhesive can be used in place of glue. It contains no moisture and causes no mess. It is available in rolls and sheets with backing paper. Acid-free versions are available, as well as repositionable and permanent types. Double-sided foam tape has some thickness to it, so is useful as a support for your paper sculpture.

## REMOVABLE ADHESIVES

Removable adhesives come as putty, clear sticky discs, or strips. They are also double-sided, can stay in place for a long time, and won't damage a surface when you remove them. The sticky discs come in different thicknesses, so they work well as supports when assembling layers. All types can be used in place of masking tape for mounting paper sculptures to a wall. Mounting strips and picture hanging strips are ideal for heavier paper sculptures or mounting a sculpture in a heavy-traffic or draughty area. The strips can be costly, so ensure that you read the instructions carefully, and use as directed.

Masking tape

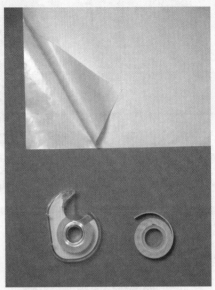
Double-sided adhesive

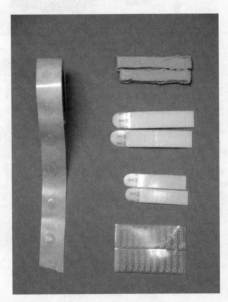
Removable adhesives

Magnetic tape

## MAGNETIC TAPE

Magnetic tape comes in a roll with a sticky back. It is good for making fridge magnets to display your paper sculpture.

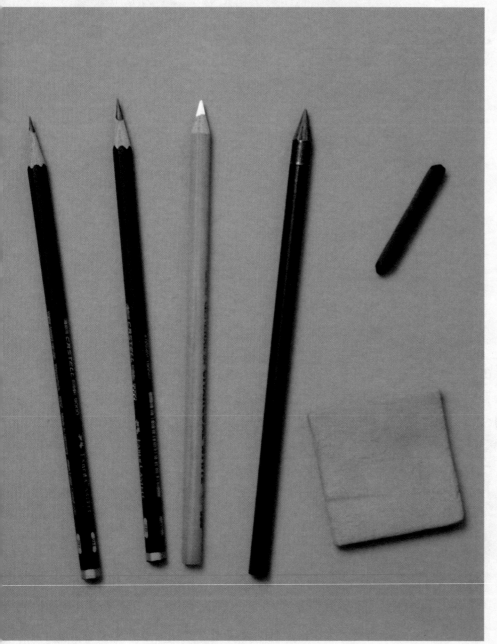

Drawing materials, pictured clockwise from left:
light pencil, dark pencil, white pencil, solid graphite, Conté crayon, kneaded eraser.

# Drawing materials

Since paper sculpture is a combination of graphic and sculptural elements, drawing and colouring materials are also frequently used to make paper sculpture. All of these items are easily obtained at art supply and craft stores, if you don't already have them.

- **Pencils:** You will need both light and dark pencils. Pencils in the H range are light; they contain harder graphite and create thinner lines. B-range pencils are darker; they contain softer graphite and create thicker lines. Use light pencil for marking and dark pencil for transferring images. It's also good to have a white pencil for use when drawing on dark paper.
- **Solid graphite:** Use this for drawing thick lines. You can also use pastel or Conté crayons instead.
- **Erasers:** A kneaded eraser (or putty rubber) works best, as it doesn't produce eraser residue and you don't need to rub away the surface of the paper. Use it to erase any pencil marks or just to clean the sculpture.

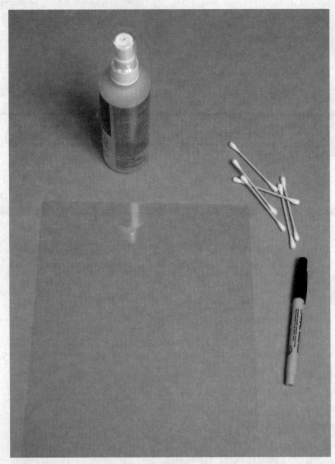

Other useful items to have to hand, pictured clockwise from top:
dry-erase board cleaner, cotton buds, permanent marker, clear overlay film.

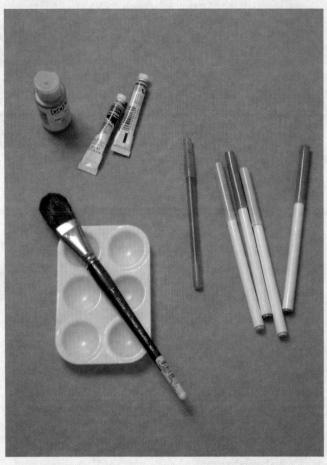

Colouring media, pictured clockwise from top left:
acrylic paint, watercolours, felt-tip pen, markers, palette, paintbrush.

# Other useful items

You will find it useful to have these items to hand when preparing your paper sculptures.

- **Permanent marker:** Use this for tracing an image onto film.
- **Dry-erase board cleaner:** Use it to erase permanent marker from film. The substitute for the marker eraser is elbow grease: vigorously rub the area with a cotton bud.

- **Cotton buds:** Useful for erasing markers or removing glue residue.
- **Clear overlay film:** This is a sheet of acetate or acetate-alternative film, and is crystal-clear. It is used for tracing photos. Freezer bags will work too.

## COLOURING MEDIA

Having various forms of colouring media will enable you to introduce colour into your artworks or customize your paper.

# Tools

You will need various cutting and shaping tools to make
a paper sculpture. These tools are readily available
at art-supply and craft stores.

## Cutting tools

You will need a good set of cutting tools
to cut your paper.

### SCISSORS

Scissors are easier and safer to use than
craft knives. Use sharp scissors for
cleaner cuts. You can cut most outlines
with scissors. Decorative scissors (also
called decorative edgers or decorative-
edge scissors) are available for cutting
repetitive geometric or abstract shapes
such as zigzags or scallops. If you are
working with children, have them use
safety scissors.

### CRAFT KNIVES

Craft knives work the best for paper
sculpture; they are ideal for cutting
all the cutting lines inside the outline.
Craft knives come in a pen shape
with a wedge-like blade. The blade will
become dull over time, and may break
easily, so have plenty of spare blades
to hand when working on a project.
Craft-knife blades are not very strong,
so you may find it easier to use a utility
knife to cut mat board. Always use a
sharp blade; it makes cutting much
easier and cleaner.

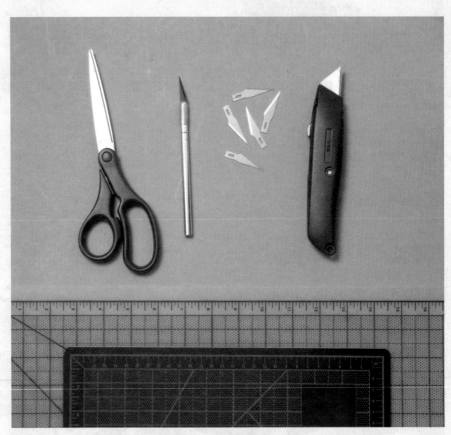

Having a range of cutting tools will enable you to cut your projects most effectively.
Always use a cutting mat for safety and to protect furniture.

### CUTTING MAT

A cutting mat is a board that is made of
self-healing material. When you cut the
surface, the damaged area will reform
(although over a long period of time
the mat eventually loses that property).
A cutting mat is a must-have for paper
cutting. They come in a variety of sizes
and colours with grids.

# Shaping tools

Shaping tools will be an essential part of your paper-sculpture toolkit.

## AWL

An awl is a long pointed tool used for scoring, curling and puncturing paper. You can also use it as a glue applicator. A knitting needle can make a good substitute for a curling tool. The back of a craft knife can be used for scoring.

## SPOON-TIP WOODEN BURNISHER

You can find this tool in art supply stores with the clay- or sculpture-modelling tools. It is used for embossing paper edges. The spoon-shaped tip makes a smooth curve on paper edges.

## STYLUS

This comes with single-ball or double-ball tips. There are different ball sizes to choose from. It is used for embossing small cut paper edges or patterns. It can also be used when transferring images. A metal crochet hook or a dentist's burnisher can be used as alternatives.

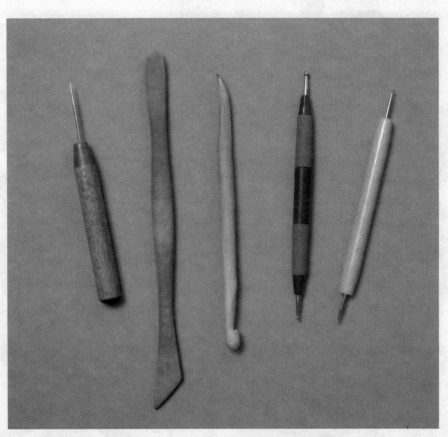

Shaping tools, pictured left to right: awl, two types of burnisher, two types of stylus.

## TOOLS FOR CURLING

Any tool that is long, smooth, rigid and round will do the job, such as the body of an awl, a craft knife handle or the shaft of a pencil. Fingers are ideal too!

# Guides

These tools will help you cut, score or draw straight or curvy lines and circles.

## METAL RULER

A metal ruler is used for drawing, measuring, scoring or cutting straight lines. Some metal rulers come with a safety guard.

## FRENCH CURVE AND FLEXIBLE CURVE

These tools are used to draw or score curvy lines. A French curve is made from rigid plastic, and has many different curves. A flexible curve is a flexible length of plastic that can be bent to create the curves you need. It comes in different lengths. If you don't have these curves, make an additional copy of the template that has a curved scoring line, secure it on a piece of heavy cardstock and cut the scoring line. Remove the template, and use the curved edge as a guide for scoring lines.

## CIRCLE TEMPLATES

These can be found on set squares or rulers and are helpful when you need to draw perfect circles. Coins, bowls or dishes work well, too.

## TAPE MEASURE

A tape measure can be helpful for measuring your display area or when working on a large piece.

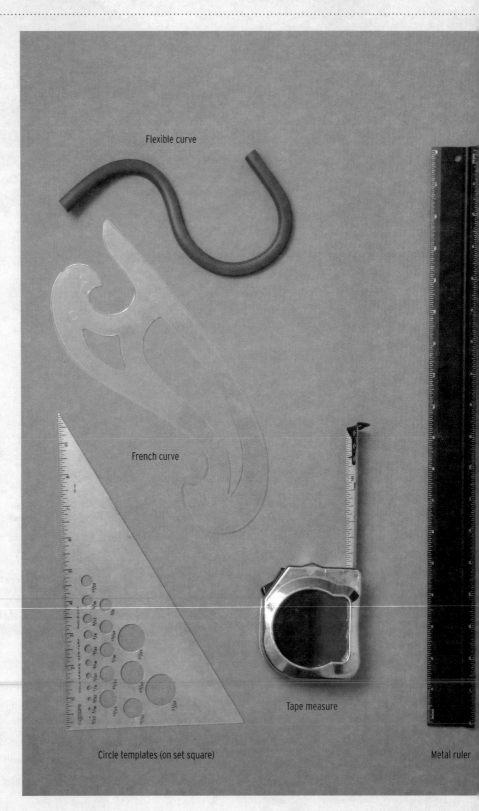

Flexible curve

French curve

Tape measure

Circle templates (on set square)

Metal ruler

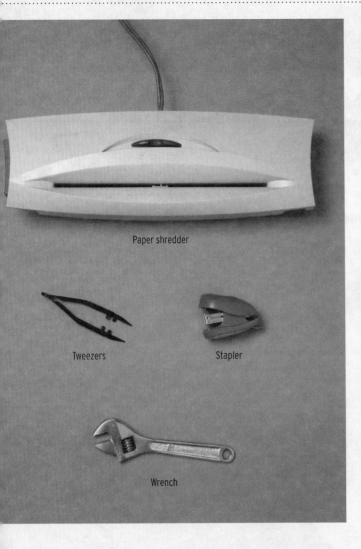

Paper shredder

Tweezers

Stapler

Wrench

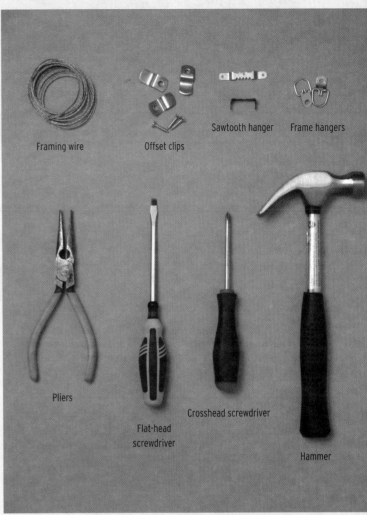

Framing wire

Offset clips

Sawtooth hanger

Frame hangers

Pliers

Flat-head
screwdriver

Crosshead screwdriver

Hammer

# Other useful tools

- **Tweezers:** Helpful when working on a small piece.
- **Stapler:** Used for securing multiple layers of paper.
- **Paper shredder:** Good for shredding large amounts of paper uniformly and quickly for use in projects.

- **Hardware:** A screwdriver, hammer, wrench, framing wire, pliers, frame hangers and offset clips are all items used for projects in this book.

## SAFETY

Some of these tools can be dangerous; use them with caution. If you have children, explain the danger of the tools and keep them out of their reach. When making paper sculptures with children, monitor them at all times, and use safer substitutes, such as safety scissors.

# Techniques

Although paper sculptures can look magical, there isn't any
trickery to the techniques; the magic is in your imagination,
in the paper and in the labour. There are several stages to
making a paper sculpture: you need to design the piece, separate
the layers, sculpt, assemble and then display the artwork.

## Designing the sculpture

The first thing you need is a 2D image of your paper sculpture. This image not only visualizes your idea, but is used for the templates. Animals, flowers, people, architecture, machines and text are all great themes for paper sculpture.

You can design a paper sculpture by drawing your own image or by tracing an image. Both techniques are explored below. Think about how you will display your work, and decide on the background shape and size accordingly. Some of the materials may be limited in size or colour, so research the materials you intend using before starting the design.

### DRAWING THE DESIGN

Make some quick, rough sketches of your subject with different layouts and environments. When you have a sketch you like, develop it in more detail. The clearer the outline of each shape, the easier it is to translate it into paper sculpture. Your design needs to include well-defined shapes of the basic features of the subject and one or more separable components. Study the subject in detail: the better you know it, the easier it is to draw and also to modify your design.

Pretty much anything you can draw can be turned into a paper sculpture, but if your design features something like stick figures or words and letters written with thin lines, you will need to modify the design, as all the shapes you cut out will need to have a reasonable amount of surface area. One way to create surface around thin lines is to redraw the lines with a broader-sized medium such as graphite pencil.

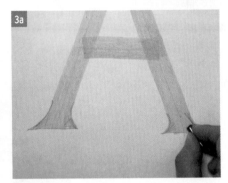

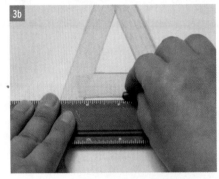

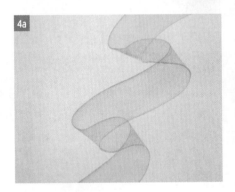

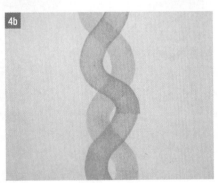

## You will need:
- Solid graphite pencil
- 1 sheet of paper
- Something to provide a soft, smooth surface such as a phone book or thick layer of newspapers

## USING A GRAPHITE PENCIL

1 Cut the graphite pencil down to the width you want your boldface letters to be (1a). Peel the protective coating off the graphite. Rub the graphite against some scrap paper until the rounded edge flattens a little (1b).

2 Put a sheet of paper on a soft, smooth surface such as a phone book (this will ensure an even coverage of graphite). Roughly write a letter with the tip of the graphite (2a). Place your graphite on the paper flat side down, and start drawing lines with horizontal, vertical, diagonal and curved lines, using the pre-written letter as a guide (2b). You can control the consistency of the thickness by changing the angle of the graphite.

3 Once you have the basic letter shape, you can modify it the way you want. Add or take away shades here and there. Define the outlines of the letter with the tip of the graphite (3a). Use a ruler for guidance if you want straight lines in your letter shape (3b).

4 This method works well if you want to create ribbon effects (4a) or braid patterns (4b).

## TRACING FROM A PHOTOGRAPH

Not everyone can draw, but tracing an image from a photograph is an equally effective way to make a design. You can use pictures from your family album, magazines, books, newspapers or the Internet. Tracing from a photograph does not mean you are being less creative; you can make the design your own by compositing it with other images, or using a creative composition.

You will need:
- 1 clear photograph that is large enough to trace
- 1 sheet of clear overlay film
- Masking tape
- Fine-tip permanent marker
- Dry-erase board cleaner
- Cotton buds and/or a paper towel

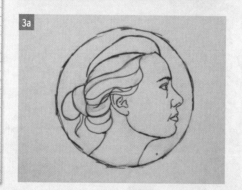

**Tip:** To save an important photo, make a photocopy of the original and use that instead.

**1** Place a sheet of clear overlay film on your work surface. Put your photograph face down on the film. Secure the photo with masking tape (1a). Flip it so that the film side faces you. With the marker, roughly draw a shape around the image you want to trace (1b); this will form the frame for the sculpture.

**2** Start by tracing the most important features first, then move on to the details (2a). Try to simplify and define each element as much as possible. Omit or add features if you like. If you make a mistake, put a drop of board cleaner on a cotton bud and dab it on the spot, then rub it with a clean, dry cotton bud (2b). (You can use a paper towel for a larger surface.)

**3** Whether you are drawing or tracing, determining the most major and prominent features is important. Mark any interesting textures on the plan with simple indications. Don't worry about putting in shadows or details; you just need a clear line drawing that shows definite shapes (3a). After the drawing or tracing is complete, photocopy it, adjusting the size if necessary. You will now make a master template, which you will use for separating and assembling layers (see pages 26 and 35).

## ADDING COLOURS TO YOUR DESIGN

Paper sculptures mainly consist of white objects against a white background; white objects against a coloured background; coloured objects against a white background and coloured objects against a coloured background. It is best to use light colours for objects. The lighter the colour is, the more light it reflects. Lighter colours show more detail, and give the object more depth. Also, solid colours work better than patterns, which tend to make the sculpture look flat.

If you are making a colourful design, there are two ways to decide on a colour scheme. One method is to secure a sheet of tracing paper over your master template and experiment using media such as coloured pencils, felt-tip pens or crayons. Take the colour scheme you like to your local art supply store, and buy the papers that most closely match your colour scheme. The other method is to check what colours are available in local stores or online first, and then plan your colour scheme accordingly.

White object on a white background

White object on a coloured background

Coloured object on a white background

Coloured object on a coloured background

Colouring with felt-tip pen

Custom-coloured paper

### CUSTOM-COLOURED PAPER

For some projects, you may not be able to find the right coloured paper, in which case you can make your own. I usually colour my paper first and then cut and shape it. It is not a good idea to use a wet medium on already shaped paper because it will alter the paper form. Let the colouring medium dry completely before cutting the paper. Paint will often warp paper, but the warped surface can get flattened out by sculpting. Avoid using any medium that can be smudged.

# Separating layers

Once you have your master template ready, you will need cutting templates that you can cut from. Some paper sculptures have only one layer, in which case you can just use the master template as the cutting template. However, if your design has multiple components, you need to separate them into individual layers. See which layer comes on top and which layer comes behind. If it is not obvious, you need to make a creative decision. In most of the projects in this book, I have separated the layers for you. I recommend that you practise on your own, using my layers as guides, to learn how the process works.

Master template

## You will need:
- Master template
- Tracing paper
- Masking tape
- Pencil
- Eraser

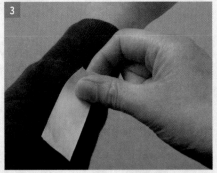

1 Secure a sheet of tracing paper over the master template with one hand; use tape to keep it in place if needed. In this example, I have used the master template for project 14: fish pond (see page 179). Trace the see-through outlines of the top layers (1a). Move or replace the tracing paper, so that a clean area lies on the next layer to be traced (1b).

2 Now you need to imagine that the previously separated layer is not there any more. Some layers under the top layers have complete outlines, but some do not, like the example shown (2a). Where the layers do not have a complete outline, you need to extend and fill in the incomplete or broken lines in order to complete the shape. Create a big enough surface on the layer, so that other layers can be attached to it (2b).

3 After you have traced all the layers to make cutting templates, secure each template on the assigned paper with a few pieces of masking tape. Sometimes you need less tacky tape to keep the paper from tearing when the tape is removed. Simply dab the tape on your skin or clothing a few times until it loses some tackiness (3).

# Shaping the paper

This is probably the most enjoyable part of paper sculpture. All your layers are separated, ready to be cut and shaped. Remember that paper sculpture is a handcraft, so the cuts will show imperfections and the creases may not be straight. Such imperfections are part of the craft's charm.

Cutting is the most basic technique to shape paper. You can make a piece of paper sculpture through cutting alone. There are two ways to cut layers using templates. Firstly, you can transfer a reversed template onto the back of the paper. Do this by tracing the template on a sheet of tracing paper with a dark, soft pencil. Place your paper for the sculpture face down. Place the tracing paper on top of the paper with the traced side facing down, so that the graphite makes contact with the paper for the sculpture. Use a burnisher or a stylus to burnish the tracing paper along the pencilled trace. Then cut the paper along the traced outlines. Secondly, you can secure the template to the front of the paper with masking tape, and cut both the template and the paper at the same time. In this book, we use the second technique for most projects.

The cutting templates provided in this book are lightly shaded so you can see where your blade made cuts. The cutting lines are marked as heavy solid lines (A); embossing or debossing lines as thinner solid lines (B), and scoring lines are marked as broken lines (C).

Cutting, embossing or debossing, and scoring lines

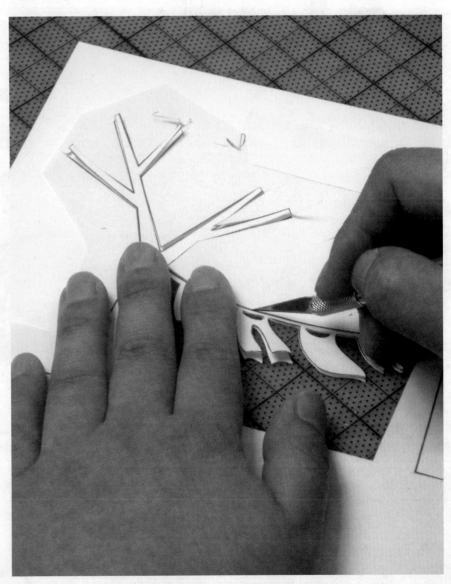

The template is secured to the paper and cut at the same time.

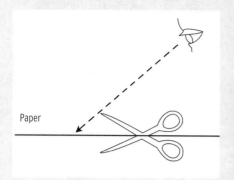

Straight cut with scissors

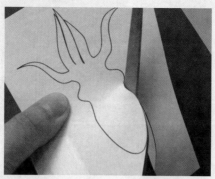

Curvy cut with scissors

## CUTTING WITH SCISSORS

Use scissors to cut the outlines if you feel more comfortable using them instead of a craft knife. Hold the paper and the template together firmly.

### Making a long straight cut

Position the paper and the scissors straight in front of you. Place the scissors on the cutting line at a right angle to the paper. Look ahead of the scissor blade (not the point it is cutting) and keep lining up the tip of the scissor blade with the cutting line while you are cutting the paper (see the diagram on the top left).

### Making a curvy cut

Slowly rotate the paper in the opposite direction of the curve with your other hand while cutting the outline.

### Making an inside corner cut

Cut both of the cutting lines from outside of the corner towards the inside corner.

Inside corner cut with scissors

## CUTTING WITH A CRAFT KNIFE

Even if you use scissors to cut the outlines, there are many cases in which you need to make cuts inside the outlines. This is when you need to use a craft knife, as it can reach the areas that scissors can't. You can also use a craft knife to cut mat board or foam board.

A sharp blade is a must. If the blade is sharp enough, you won't need to apply much pressure to cut the paper; just make a few gentle strokes per cut. If you feel you are putting too much pressure on the knife, stop and release the pressure by relaxing your hand for a second, then start cutting again.

Whether you make a straight or a curvy cut, keep the blade at a right angle to the surface, especially when you cut heavyweight paper, mat board or foam board. When you make intricate cuts, keep checking on the back to see that the paper is being cut through or whether any cutting lines are missing.

### Making a straight cut

Use a metal ruler to cut straight lines. Try to place the ruler inside the shape, and keep your hand holding the knife outside the shape whenever possible. That way, if your hand slips, the shape is still safe. Make a few gentle strokes along the cutting lines. Mat board will need three or four strokes to cut through it, or as many as it takes until you feel the blade touch the cutting mat underneath.

### Making an outside corner cut

Make each cut, passing the cutting line so that the two cuts cross each other.

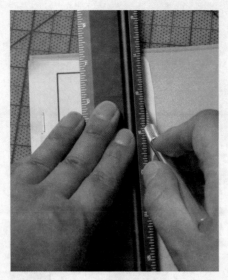
Straight cut with a craft knife

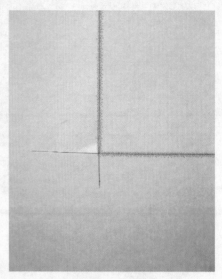
Outside corner cut with a craft knife

### Making an inside corner cut

Cut each cutting line starting from the corner. When the cutting line starts and stops at another inside corner, cut the line a little bit starting from one corner. Turn the paper, and finish cutting the rest of the line starting from the other corner.

### Making a curvy cut

Place the blade on the cutting line with one hand, and hold the paper with the other hand. As you cut the curve, slowly rotate the paper in the opposite direction of the curve. When the curves are steep, cut just a small amount at a time while you keep rotating the paper.

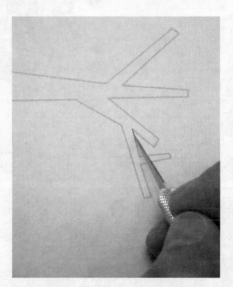
Inside corner cut with a craft knife

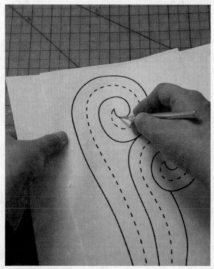
Curvy cut with a craft knife

## EMBOSSING

Embossing means to raise a surface of a pliable material. This technique is used in paper sculpture to give dimension to a piece of flat paper, creating curved edges. It is also used to apply an image or texture to the surface of the paper. Embossing is achieved by burnishing the surface with pressure on the back of the paper, usually against a piece of foam board. You need a spoon-tip wooden burnisher or a stylus craft tool, and a sheet of foam board.

### Embossing edges

Place a sheet of foam board on your work surface. Put a piece of paper face down on the foam board. Using either a burnisher or a stylus, firmly burnish the paper very close to the edges.

### Embossing with a stencil

A stencil has one or more shaped holes to guide pressure to affect only certain areas. You can make a stencil, or use a found object such as metal mesh or a colander. To make a stencil, you can use a hole punch, or draw and cut a hole with the shape you need on a piece of heavy paper. To emboss a pattern onto paper using a stencil, place the stencil face down. Place a sheet of paper on the stencil, also face down. You can either burnish the paper with a burnisher to expose the patterns, or use a light source to locate the pattern. Then use a stylus to trace the edges of the pattern. You don't need foam board for this. Turn the paper over to reveal the embossed pattern.

Embossing with a wooden burnisher

Edges of the stencil traced with a stylus

Front of embossed paper

### Embossing without a stencil

On the back of the paper against a piece of foam board, firmly burnish the surface with a stylus as if you are drawing a pattern. You can do this with or without a pattern template.

Embossed paper without using a stencil

Debossed paper

### Debossing

Debossing is the opposite of embossing, when pressure is applied to the front of the paper to make the surface recess. In paper sculpture, embossing or debossing is also used instead of scoring to create smooth creases in the paper rather than sharp, crisp ones.

## CRUMPLING

This technique shows off the charm of paper. It can be used to make rocks and to weather paper to make it look aged. Lightweight paper is easier to work with. Just crumple the paper once, then flatten it out. Crumple it more in a different direction until you get enough creases. Try crumpling tissue paper, too; it gives an interesting texture and dimension to the paper.

Lightweight paper is best for crumpling.

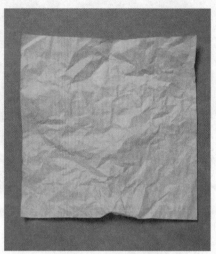

Flatten your paper after crumpling it just once, so you can see if it's creased enough for what you want; if not, repeat the process.

## SCORING

Scoring is one of the most frequently used techniques in paper sculpture. It breaks the fibre in the paper neatly, making it easier to create a clean crease. The cleaner the scoring line is, the better the crease looks. This technique can be used to create sharp creases for abstract shapes, architecture or machines. Just a slight bend creates a pleasing shadow that shows off the signature characteristics of low-relief paper sculpture.

For scoring paper, use a sharp-pointed tool, such as an awl or the back of a craft knife, plus a ruler or French curve and a cutting mat. Place the paper on the cutting mat and position the awl or the back of the craft knife on the paper. Tilt the tool in the direction in which you want to work so the dull side touches the paper. Move the tool, keeping it tilted and firmly pressed against the paper. Use a ruler to score a straight line and a French curve to score curves.

When scoring, keep the awl tilted and press down firmly as you move the tool.

## CURLING

This technique is used to make curves on paper edges, or to shape a flat piece of paper into curls. It creates bigger curves than embossing. If you plan to use curling techniques, it's good to add a little more room on the layers when you separate them. You need an object such as an awl, pencil or the handle of a craft knife to curl the paper round.

### Curling waves

Curl a section of a piece of paper in one direction (a). Turn the paper 180 degrees. Place the tool right next to the previous curl, and curl the paper in the opposite direction from the previous curl (b). Repeat, turning and curling as you need.

### Short curls

To make curls upwards, place the tool on the front edge of the paper. Hold the tool and the paper firmly between your thumb and index finger. Turn the tool and the paper together towards you (a).

### Big curls

To make curls upwards, place the curling tool on the front of the paper away from the edge and put your thumb on the tool. Support the tool from the back of the paper with your index finger. Move the tool flush against the paper towards the edge in a scraping motion (a).

To make curls downwards, place the curling tool against the back edge of the paper and firmly hold the curling tool and the paper between your thumb and index finger. Turn the tool and the paper together away from you (b).

To make curls downwards, place the tool on the back of the paper away from the edge and put your thumb on the paper where the tool is. Move the curling tool flush against the paper towards the edge in a scraping motion (b).

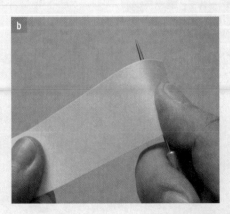

## TEARING

Tearing paper creates a spontaneous and natural look, and shows off some of its charming idiosyncrasies. Tearing can be used to make mountains, animal fur, fuzzy plants and decorative edges.

Torn edges vary depending on paper type, so experiment with different kinds. For example, machine-made paper has rough edges when it is torn. The fibres in the pulp create a grain, and paper will tear straighter if it is torn in the direction of the grain. Tear two sheets of the same kind of paper lengthwise and crosswise and see how different the tears look. Also, try tearing the paper away from you and towards you. You will see that when you tear paper towards you, the remaining paper will have a rougher edge on the front. The torn-away piece will have the rougher edge on the back.

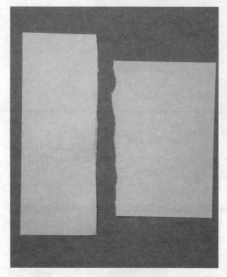

A paper tear will look different depending on whether you've torn it lengthwise or crosswise...

... and away from or towards you.

**Tip:** You can use either side of the punctured paper for your projects.

## PUNCTURING

This technique can be used to make features such as eyes, flower parts, stitches, and machinery. You will need a sharp-pointed tool, such as an awl, a thick, soft surface, such as a sheet of foam board or cardboard, and a cutting mat. Place the sheet of cardboard or foam board underneath the paper and puncture the paper with a sharp tool.

Puncture paper using a sharp-pointed tool with a thick, soft surface underneath.

Repeated puncturing can create texture, such as the pollen in these paper flowers.

# Assembly

This is the stage where your two-dimensional image comes to life. All of the cut and shaped pieces of paper now need to be put together. If your sculpture is composed of multiple components with more than one layer, assemble the components first. Use your templates as guides. Use an appropriate adhesive for the purpose. You can directly attach one piece to another, or use supports.

## SUPPORTS

A support is a small piece that connects two pieces of paper while providing a sense of space.

**Foam board supports**

Cut the foam board into a smaller shape of the layer that needs to be supported.

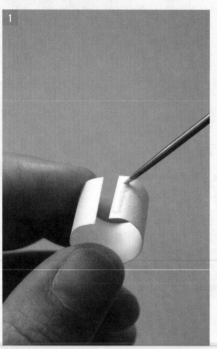

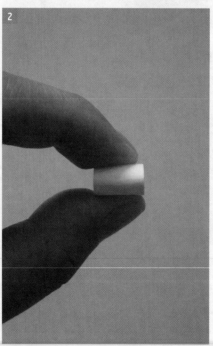

## LOOPED SUPPORTS

1 Cut a strip out of the same paper that the layer you are supporting is cut from. Curl the strip with an awl and glue the ends to make a loop (1).

2 You can reduce the height by pressing the top and bottom. You can also raise the height by pressing both sides of the loop (2).

**Dimensional adhesives**

Some double-sided adhesives such as sticky discs and double-sided foam tape have a thickness to them (see page 15). Cut them to the size you require.

## ASSEMBLING LAYERS

The diagram on the right is an example of how to assemble layers. Templates for the petal layers are provided on page 181. See also the detailed instructions on page 128.

Place petal 2 on the master template, matching the guidelines shown on the illustration. Position and attach the top layer (petal 1) to petal 2. These two attached layers are now the top layer. Put to one side. Now position petal 3 on the master template, and attach the previously assembled top layer to it. Continue assembling layers, following the diagram through to petal 6. Sometimes, unlike the example shown here, no part of the upper layer extends beyond the edges of the layer below. If this is the case you need to use the master template as a reference to position the layer in the right place.

If you need to remove the glued paper (this works if you have used water-soluble glue, see page 14), slightly dampen the glued area with a cotton bud, and wait for a minute or two. Gently lift the paper to see if it is still stuck. If necessary, repeat the process until the glue loosens. Clean up any glue residue on the sculpture. Slightly dampen a cotton bud, dab it on the glue residue, and immediately and gently wipe and dry it off with a dry cotton bud. If you used colour paper, test it on a scrap piece left over from making the sculpture.

If you would like to lay it out first to see what the finished sculpture looks like before permanently fixing the layers in place, use repositionable adhesive for temporary assembly of the sculpture. Make any necessary changes, and then use permanent adhesive.

# Presentation and display

Paper sculpture often takes a lot of time to create, and it is fragile and sensitive to humidity and ultraviolet light. Therefore the best way to keep it safe and to cherish it for a long time is to frame it.

## TRADITIONAL FRAMES

The kind of frame that is used for three-dimensional artwork has various names, such as a deep frame, a box frame, a shadow frame and a shadow-box frame. There are ready-made frames and there are custom frames.

Ready-made frames come with a standard-sized frame, a glazed panel that is either glass or acrylic, a pre-cut mat and a backing board. They are usually pretty affordable, but don't offer many options.

For custom frames, there are many styles and colours to choose from in whatever sizes you need. However these are much more expensive than ready-made frames.

A range of framing options can be used for your paper sculptures, from the traditional to the more unusual.

Components of a ready-made frame

## Importance of rabbet depth

When looking at frames, it is easy to get confused between the frame height and the rabbet depth (see the diagram right). The rabbet depth is the recess of the back inside edge of the frame into which the artwork fits. It is best to choose a frame with a rabbet depth that is a little deeper than your artwork. Many ready-made frames now have grooves on the rabbets and swing braces on the frame backing board, so you won't need a special framing tool. The grooves are convenient, but you can ignore them if necessary; sometimes you need the space more than the convenience. Some ready-made frames come with spacers built in.

If you are going to use a ready-made frame, shop around before designing your paper sculpture to see what kind of frames are available and how deep they are. Then you can plan your paper sculpture accordingly.

Rabbet grooves in the back of a ready-made frame

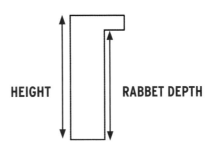

Profile

HEIGHT          RABBET DEPTH

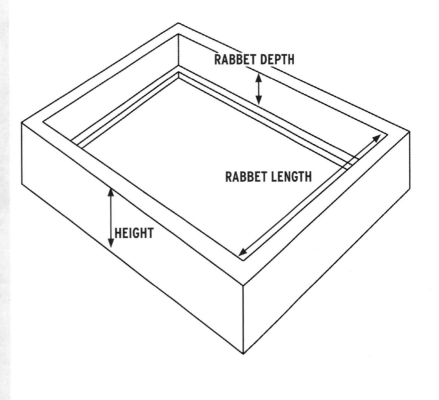

Back of frame

RABBET DEPTH

RABBET LENGTH

HEIGHT

## Making frame spacers

To frame a dimensional artwork, you need frame spacers to keep the glazing in place, providing a space in between the glazing and an unmatted artwork. Frame spacers can also be used when a part of the artwork is displayed over the mat to enhance the 3-D effect. If all the the artwork stays behind the mat you will not need frame spacers.

### You will need:

- Blanket
- 1 sheet of foam board, a little longer than your frame, and ³⁄₁₆in (5mm) thick
- Knife
- Metal ruler
- Double-sided tape
- Pencil
- Cutting mat

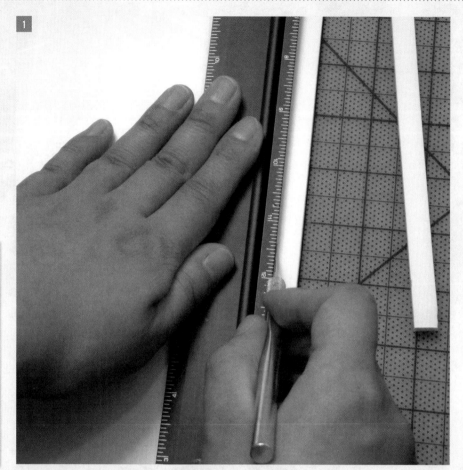

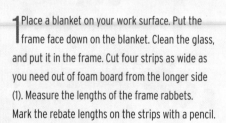

1 Place a blanket on your work surface. Put the frame face down on the blanket. Clean the glass, and put it in the frame. Cut four strips as wide as you need out of foam board from the longer side (1). Measure the lengths of the frame rabbets. Mark the rebate lengths on the strips with a pencil.

2 Take ³⁄₁₆in (5mm) away from the first measurement, and make the final markings (2a). Cut the strips to size (2b). Arrange the strips flush against the rabbets, overlapping the ends in the same direction (see diagram, page 39). On the back of each strip, apply double-sided tape, and carefully put it back in the frame (2c).

## Making mat spacers

When you mat your artwork you will need mat spacers to create a space between the artwork and mat. Mat spacers can also be used to support a layer that spans the entire frame.

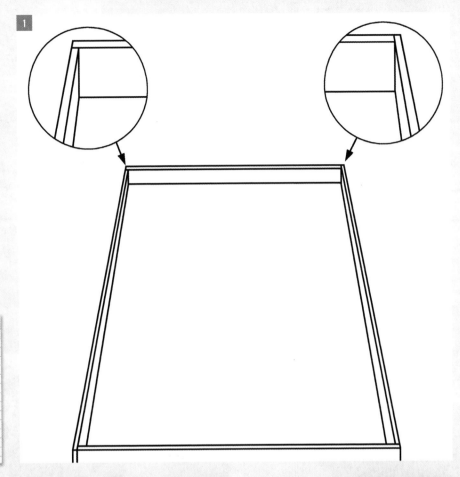

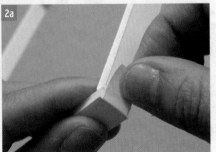

1 Cut four strips out of foam board as wide as you need. Measure the lengths of your backboard. Mark them on each strip. Take ³⁄₁₆in (5mm) away from the first measurement, and make the final markings. Cut the strips to size. Arrange the strips as shown in the diagram (1).

2 Tape the outside corners (2a) to make spacers. To attach the spacers, place the backboard on top of the strips, face down. Make sure that the mat board is placed evenly on all sides of the strips. Tape the backboard to the strips securely (2b).

## Assembling the piece in the frame

Once you have completed your artwork and the spacers are installed in the frame, you need to place the sculpture in the frame. Place the frame and the artwork face down. Measure how much the artwork sticks out (or recesses).

Now you need special hardware called offset clips. They are also called canvas clips or canvas offset clips. You can get these at hardware stores, framing shops and online stores. They are inexpensive, and come in big or small packages and many different depths, starting from $\frac{1}{8}$in (3mm). They are very useful when you need more frame depth. If your artwork sticks out about $\frac{1}{4}$in (6mm), use $\frac{1}{4}$in (6mm) offset clips, and position them upwards. If your artwork recesses by $\frac{1}{4}$in (6mm), get some $\frac{1}{4}$in (6mm) clips and position them downwards. As inexpensive, it's good to have a variety of depths to hand.

Most ready-made frames come with a sawtooth hanger, which works well for smaller frames. For larger and heavier frames, it is best to use picture frame hangers. Both types of hanger can be found at hardware or art supply stores.

Fish-pond sculpture assembled in frame

Position offset clips upwards if artwork sticks out

Position offset clips downwards if artwork recesses

## NON-TRADITIONAL FRAMES

Besides using traditional picture frames, there are other kinds of unconventional frames that you can use. Wall clocks, table clocks, clear-topped containers, pocket watches and shadow-box lockets can be great substitutes for traditional frames. They tend to be very affordable and don't require spacers. However, because you will most likely be upcycling or recycling such frames, you will need to design the paper sculpture specifically to fit in the frame.

It is usually simple to use these kinds of frames, but framing an artwork in a circular wall clock – a technique used in the Dog portrait project (see page 110) – can be tricky. Here is one way to do it.

### You will need:
- Circular clock
- Pencil or marker
- Screwdriver
- Masking tape
- Scissors or craft knife

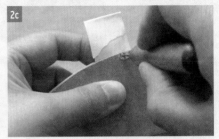

1 Before dismantling the clock, place the frame straight and face down, so that the clock hanger stays vertical. Mark the location of the very top screw hole on the clock frame right above where the clock face sits (1). Take the clock face out. Dismantle the clock parts. Leave the hanger on the back of the clock face.

2 On the clock face, mark the centreline with two pieces of masking tape, one on the twelve o'clock and one on the six o'clock (2a). Position your sculpture on the clock face, using the tape markings as a guide (2b). Hold the sculpture and the clock face altogether, and make a small hole on the sculpture through the very top screw hole of the clock face (2c).

3 Cut a small notch on your sculpture, passing the marking a little (3a). Put the sculpture in the clock frame, aligning the notch with the marked screw hole on the clock frame (3b). Remove the tape, and place the clock face in the frame, matching the top screw holes (3c). Screw the clock face in the clock frame (3d).

## HANGING THE FRAMED ARTWORK

**1** Put the blanket on your worksurface and place the frame on it. Arrange the offset clips evenly on the frame, and screw them in with a screwdriver (1a). If there is a gap between the clip and the artwork, put a sheet of paper or mat board in between. Screw the hangers in about one-third along the vertical length of the frame (1b).

**2** Pull the wire about half the width of the frame, and bend it (2a). Thread the wire loop through the hanger (2b), and then put the short side of the wire through the wire loop (2c). Twist the short wire along the long wire about halfway along its length (2d), then twist the remaining wire back to where the hanger is (2e).

**3** Lightly hold the long wire against the other hanger with one hand. Pull the wire with your other hand until the centre of the wire reaches just under the frame moulding (3a). Bend the wire where it meets the hanger, and keep pulling the wire to about half of the width of the frame. Cut the wire, and repeat the remaining directions in step 2 (3b).

## You will need:

- Blanket
- 1 wooden deep frame, with the artwork in the frame
- 8 or more offset clips, the same depth as the difference in depth between your artwork and frame
- Screws
- Screwdriver
- Sheet of paper or mat board (optional)
- 2 picture-frame hangers
- Picture-framing wire
- Pliers

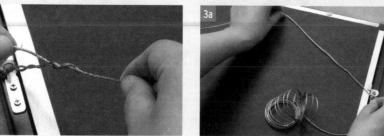

## MOUNTING SCULPTURES WITHOUT FRAMES

A paper sculpture doesn't need to be framed if it's for temporary display; it should still last long enough to enjoy for years. You can make greeting cards for all kinds of occasions using paper-sculpture techniques, and you can decorate your rooms for special occasions, or for seasonal decor, by installing paper sculptures directly on the wall.

When my son was born, I decorated his nursery with paper sculptures, all mounted by pieces of removable adhesive. They stayed on the wall for a few years until I took them down to change the decor.

Some types of removable adhesive can be a little tricky to use and costly if you make mistakes. Masking tape is the easiest to use and the most cost-effective for temporary display. Whatever you use, it is best to choose a display spot where there is little traffic, humidity or draughts, and no direct sunlight.

1 Cut a few inches of masking tape. Make several loops, sticky side out (1).

2 Put them on the back of the paper sculpture close to the upper edge, and press the sculpture against the wall (2). If you need to reposition it, take the tape off the wall by pulling the tape and the paper together, but not the paper alone. When the sculpture is positioned, secure the sculpture with plenty of looped masking tape.

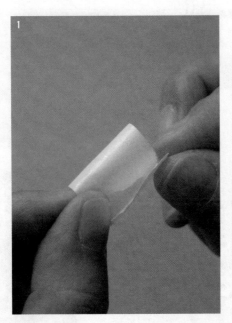

# Paper
# Sculptures

# Butterfly

The inspiration for this project came from paint colour
swatches. If you have ever done any home decorating,
or are planning to, you may already have some of these;
otherwise they are free to pick up from DIY stores.
This project is very easy, and has many potential end uses.
Put it in a shadow-box locket to make a colourful accessory,
as shown here; use it for scrapbooking or to make a greeting
card; or make lots of butterflies in different colour
combinations and arrange them on a wall for decoration.

# You will need:

## Materials

- Templates on page 140, sized to fit in your shadowbox locket (NB: you will not need to photocopy them if the templates at 100% fit your frame; you can transfer the images straight from the book)
- Paint colour sample cards in 5 different shades
- 1 sheet of tracing paper, 9 x 12in (23 x 30.5cm), or A4 size
- Masking tape
- Single-sided shadowbox locket, at least 1½in (3.8cm) in diameter and ¼in (6mm) deep, and chain
- Glue
- Dimensional double-sided adhesive

## Tools

- Scissors
- Dark pencil
- Stylus
- Awl

# Instructions:

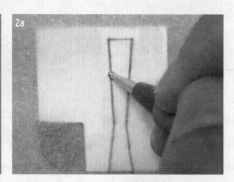

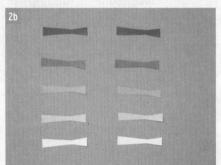

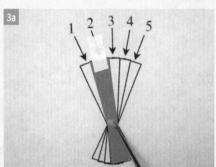

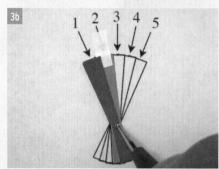

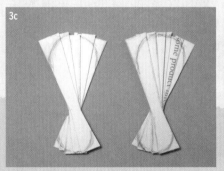

1 Cut away any type or white borders on the coloured side of your paint samples, so you are left with a solid colour (1a). Fold the paper in half, wrong side out (1b). On a piece of tracing paper, trace template 1 on page 140 using a dark pencil.

2 Place the tracing paper on a colour sample, traced side down (2a). With a stylus, burnish the see-through pencil lines onto the sample. Repeat for the others. Darken the pencil lines on the tracing paper as needed. Cut the shapes out by cutting through both layers of the folded paper at

the same time. Sort the shapes by colour, placing them in order from darkest to lightest, and divide the shapes into two sets (2b).

3 Take the second darkest shape and place it in position 2 on template 2 with low-tack masking tape (see page 26) (3a). With the awl, apply a thin layer of glue to its axis. Put the darkest shape in position 1, pressing it down on the axis of the previous shape (3b). Remove the tape and put the pieces aside. Now secure the third darkest shape to position 3 on the template and glue the pieces

you just set aside to its axis. Remove the tape. Continue until you have completed all layers for both wings. Trim the wings into a curved shape (3c).

4 Arrange the wings in the locket, then glue the two sets together on the axis (4a). Cut a thin strip about 2in (5cm) long out of any colour to make the antennae. Fold it in half, and twist it to about halfway. Curl the antennae and glue them to the wings (4b). To finish, put a piece of dimensional double-sided adhesive on the back of the butterfly, and stick it down inside your locket.

# Snake

One of the wonderful characteristics of paper sculpture is that
it can mimic a wide range of materials. In this project, paper is
used to look like metal. You could either use a metallic paper,
which is available as cardstock or gift-wrapping paper, or
paint ordinary paper with metallic paint, as I have done here.
I have chosen to display this paper sculpture in an upcycled
pocket watch to give it a Steampunk feel, but you could
choose an alternative method of display from among
the various options shown in this book.

# You will need:

## Materials

- Templates on page 141, sized to fit in your frame. (NB: the templates do not need to be photocopied if 100% scale will fit in your frame - you can transfer the images straight from the book)
- 1 sheet of white lightweight to medium-weight cardstock
- Metallic paint
- Paintbrush
- 1 sheet of tracing paper, 9 x 12in (23 x 30.5cm), or A4 size
- Masking tape
- Mesh object, such as a metal mesh tray used as a desk tidy or a wire cooling rack, to use as a stencil
- 1 sheet of foam board, 8½ x 11in (21.6 x 28cm), for embossing
- Glue
- Dimensional double-sided adhesive
- 1 pocket watch, at least 1½in (4.5cm) in diameter and with the mechanism removed, to use as the display case

## Tools

- Dark pencil
- Stylus
- Spoon-tip wooden burnisher
- Craft knife

# Instructions:

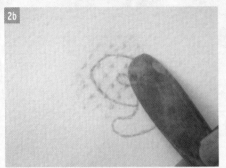

1 Take the white cardstock and colour it on one side with metallic paint (1a). Let the paint dry. With masking tape, secure a sheet of tracing paper to the head, body and tail templates (1b). Trace the cutting lines using a dark pencil. Secure the tracing paper, traced side down, on the back of the painted paper. Using a stylus, burnish the see-through lines onto the white side of the painted paper.

2 With masking tape, secure the painted paper onto the mesh, metallic side down (2a). With a burnisher, vigorously burnish the paper until you see the mesh pattern start to appear (2b). With a stylus, trace the edges of the holes with gentle pressure; experiment on a piece of scrap paper to see how much pressure you need to apply.

3 Using the craft knife, cut the paper along the pencil line. On the white side of each piece, carefully emboss the edges with a fine-tipped stylus. If the pattern becomes flattened, define it by burnishing the grooves on the front (3a), and emboss on the back.

4 Place the head layer of the snake onto the master template, and put a little glue on the tip of the base (4a). Place the body layer onto the master template, overlapping it with the head layer. Using a stylus, press the grooves down on the glued area (4b). Make sure the coil moves freely in a springy motion.

5 Take the tail layer and repeat the process as above (5a). Cut a small piece of paper for the tongue and glue it to the head. Put some dimensional double-sided adhesive on the back of the snake, and place it inside the case (5b). Reassemble the case.

# Pop-up card

Pop-up engineering and paper sculpture are closely related
to each other in terms of materials, playing with dimensions,
and structures. This greeting card uses a combination of paper
cutting and a very simple pop-up technique. You will practise
a number of cutting skills in this project; read up on them on
pages 28-9 before starting. Remember that imperfection
is okay: it is part of the charm of handmade art.

# You will need:

## Materials

- 1 photocopy of each template on pages 142-143, enlarged to 150%
- Assembly guidelines, for reference (see pages 144-146)
- 2 sheets of white medium-weight cardstock for the pop-up
- Masking tape
- 1 sheet of medium- to heavyweight cardstock, 8½ x 11in (21.6 x 28cm), in any colour for the cover
- Scrap paper
- Glue stick

## Tools

- Cutting mat
- Craft knife
- Scissors (optional)
- Metal ruler
- Awl
- Pencil
- Eraser

# Instructions:

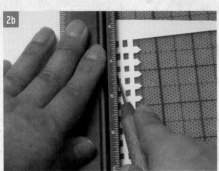

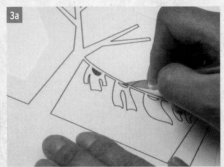

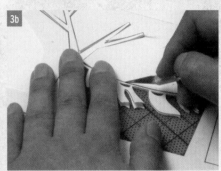

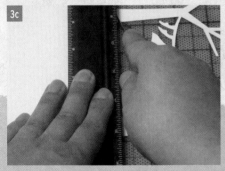

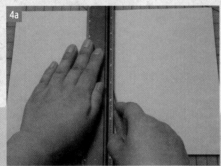

1 With masking tape, secure the fence template to a sheet of white cardstock (1a) and place it on your cutting mat. Carefully cut along all of the lines, except for the sun. Check to see if you have missed any areas by turning your paper over and looking at it from the back (1b).

2 Separate the cut pieces by gently wiggling the cut lines back and forth (2a). On the front, score the bases of the trees and the fence with an awl (2b). Roughly cut around the sun template and put it to one side to use later.

3 With the other sheet of white cardstock and the clothesline template, repeat steps 1 and 2. Cut the negative spaces on the clothing first (3a). Make multiple gentle strokes to cut the shapes, applying just a little pressure. Hold the shapes that are being cut with one hand as you cut the clothesline (3b). On the back, score the bases of the trees (3c).

4 Place your cover paper horizontally on the cutting mat. Find the middle and make a vertical score line using a ruler and an awl (4a). Fold the paper, then open it again. On the left side, lightly draw a line with a pencil, $\frac{1}{8}$in (3mm) away from the valley crease. Flip the cover so that the pencil marking is on the back of the right side of the cover. Take the sun template and secure it to the right side of the cover with a few pieces of low-tack masking tape (see page 26) (4b).

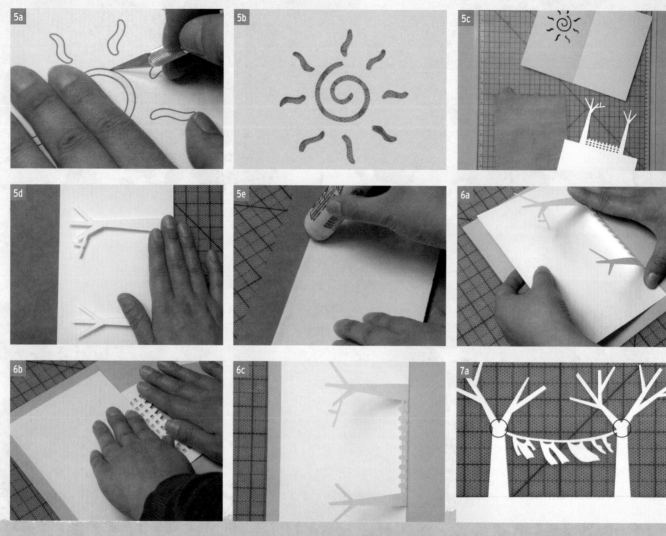

5 Cut out the shapes that make up the sun, rotating the paper as you cut the curves (5a). Carefully remove the template (5b). Now take a sheet of scrap paper, the first layer of the card that you cut out, and the cover. Place them on your work surface (5c). On the fence layer, fold the trees and the fence over (5d). Place these, trees side down, onto the sheet of scrap paper. Apply glue all around the edges (5e), making sure you keep the glue close to the edges, so that the glue doesn't show through the sun when the card is assembled.

6 Turn the fence layer over, and line up the trees and fence bases with the marking on the inside of the cover paper, centring the rectangle within the top and bottom edges of the cover (6a). Now unfold the trees and the fence and burnish the glued area with your hand (6b). Once again, fold the trees and the fence (6c).

7 On the front of the clothesline layer, apply some glue at the base of the tree branches (7a). Place the rectangle side of this layer onto the other side of the cover paper, glue side down, so that both layers of the tree bases match back to back while the two rectangles line up side by side (7b). Attach the trees together (7c) and then fold over the rectangle side of the clothesline layer (7d).

**Tip:** To make sure the card pop ups properly, the two layers need to be distanced equally from the centrefold.

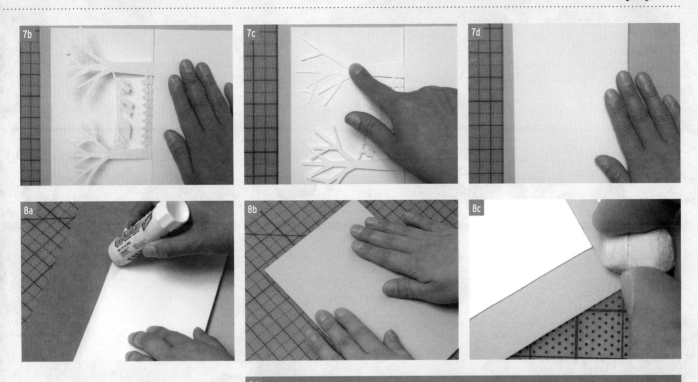

8 Place a sheet of scrap paper under the rectangle. Apply glue along the edges of the rectangle (8a) then remove the scrap paper. Now fold the cover paper over the rectangle and burnish the glued area with your hand (8b). Unfold the card and erase any visible pencil markings on the coloured paper (8c). To complete the card, cut out some leaf shapes and a bird from the white paper and glue them onto the trees as shown (8d).

# Music plaque

The musical notes for 'Mary had a little lamb' form the subject for this fun project, making it ideal for decorating a nursery. Alternatively, you can choose music from your favourite song or lullaby. The music staves are made from shredded paper, so it's a good way to recycle those unwanted documents!

# You will need:

## Materials

- 1 photocopy of each template on pages 148-150, copied at 100%
- The musical notes for 'Mary had a little lamb', for reference (see page 147)
- 3 sheets of white cardstock for the lamb bodies, musical notes and bar lines
- 1 sheet of brown cardstock for the lamb heads and legs
- Masking tape
- Glue
- Foam tape
- 2 sheets of shredded white cardstock or copy paper to make the music staves

## Tools

- Cutting mat
- Stapler
- Craft knife
- Scissors (optional)
- Metal ruler
- Tweezers
- Paper shredder

# Instructions:

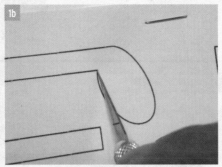

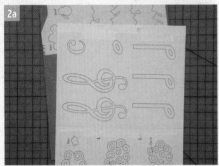

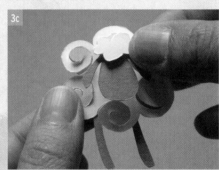

1 Stack two sheets of cardstock and fold in half. Place the bar line and the crotchet templates on the folded cardstock and staple the five layers together (1a). With the craft knife, cut the round part of the note, starting from the corner (1b). Check the back to see that the paper is completely cut through. Cut the rest of the shapes out, using a ruler as a guide for the straight edges (1c).

2 Secure each of the remaining templates to their assigned piece of paper with some masking tape (2a). Cut any cutting lines inside the outlines first before cutting the outlines (2b). When working on the fleece layers, cut each swirl outwards from the centre a little bit at a time while you rotate the paper with your other hand. Remove the templates and carefully lift the centre of each swirl with tweezers while holding down the base of the pattern (2c).

3 Position the fleece layers on the lamb base. On lambs 2 and 3, push the ears to the front through the ear slots (3a). Lift the fleece while holding the ear and the ear slot together. On the back of each fleece layer, apply a thin layer of glue on the flat surfaces, but not on the swirls. Carefully position and attach it to the base. Attach the fleece to the head of lamb 1 with a piece of foam tape (3b). Again using foam tape, attach the head to the middle of the body (3c).

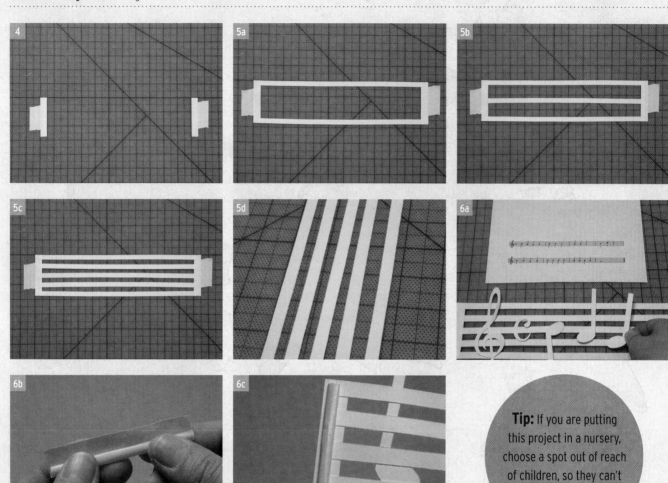

**Tip:** If you are putting this project in a nursery, choose a spot out of reach of children, so they can't pull it down.

4 To make a stave, place two of the bar lines vertically on your cutting mat, 10½in (26cm) apart. Take two pieces of low-tack masking tape (see page 26). Tape the bar lines down on the cutting mat, lining them up with the grid (4).

5 Arrange two paper strips horizontally to make the top and bottom of the stave (5a). (Note that this is the back of the stave. If you are recycling printed paper, arrange the strips accordingly.) Glue another one horizontally across the middle (5b). Attach two more strips in between to make a five-line stave (5c). Make sure that the strips are laid flat (5d) then remove the tape. Repeat to make seven more staves, or as many as you need.

6 Place the staves right side up. Using the sheet music provided on page 147 as a reference, start gluing the symbols on the staves (6a). Cut a piece of masking tape about ⅛in (3mm) shorter than the bar line and roll it lengthwise, sticky side out (6b). Make one rolled piece for every bar line. Attach them to the back of the bar lines on all of the staves (6c).

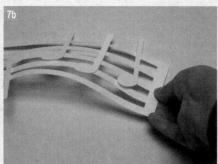

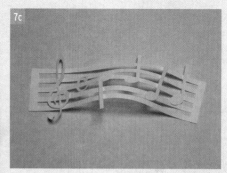

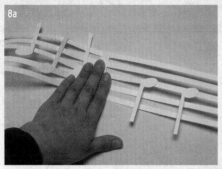

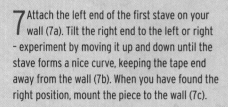

7 Attach the left end of the first stave on your wall (7a). Tilt the right end to the left or right – experiment by moving it up and down until the stave forms a nice curve, keeping the tape end away from the wall (7b). When you have found the right position, mount the piece to the wall (7c).

8 Attach the left end of the second stave to the right end of the first stave (8a). Position and attach the right end to the wall, creating a curve (8b). After all the staves are connected, attach looped masking tape to the lambs (8c) then attach them to the wall (8d). Move the lambs around until you're happy with the final effect (8e).

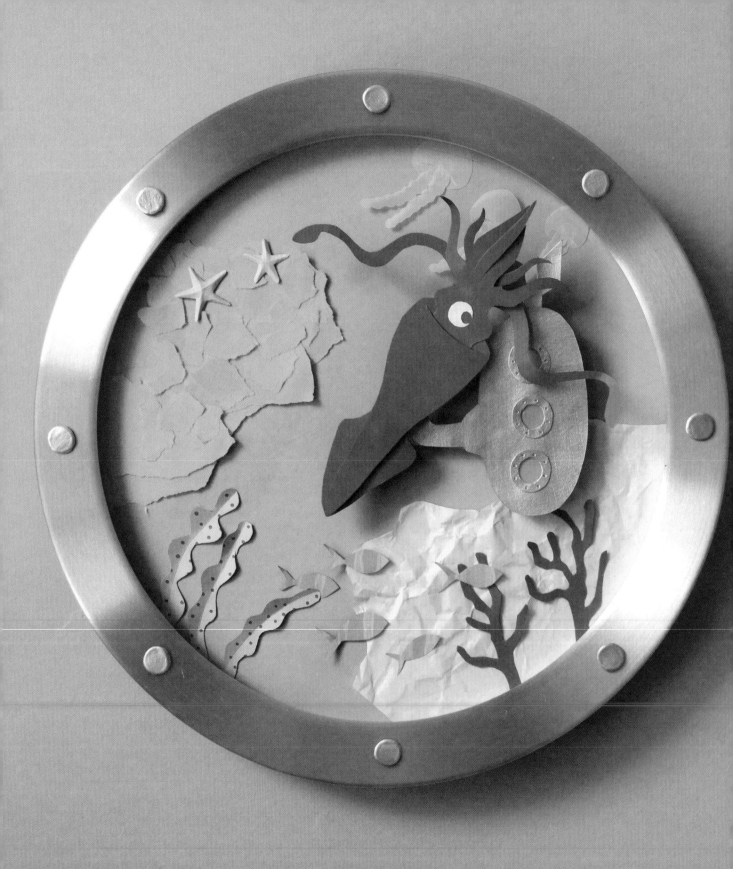

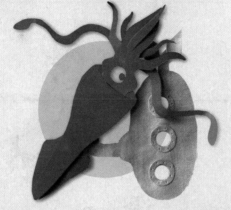

# Kraken & submarine

Children can enjoy helping to make this project. They can have fun colouring, crumpling, tearing and even simple cutting if you have a blunt-nosed pair of scissors. Why not have them draw their own version of a sea monster and marine scene, and use their design for the project? This project utilizes a clock that still has all its parts working. It is designed to be more like a mechanical toy than a functional clock, although if you add 12 bolts to the clock frame to mark the hours, you'll be able to tell the time from it too!

# You will need:

## Materials

- 1 photocopy of each template on pages 151–153, sized to fit in your clock window
- 1 sheet of paper in an aquatic colour, bigger than the clock face, for the seawater background
- Several sheets of cardstock in various colours of your choice for the sea creatures and seascape
- 1 sheet of cardstock in a metallic colour for the submarine
- 1 sheet of translucent paper such as vellum, 8½ x 11in (21.6 x 28cm), for the jellyfish and the submarine windows
- 1 sheet of foam board, 8½ x 11in (21.6 x 28cm), to use as a base for puncturing
- 1 functioning wall clock that has a gap of at least ¼in (6mm) between the face and hour hand; ideally, with a white metal-looking frame
- Foam tape, 1/16in (1.5mm) thick
- Masking tape
- Glue

## Tools

- Pencil
- Ruler
- Scissors
- Awl, or alternative pointed tool such as a knitting needle
- Craft knife
- Cutting mat
- Eraser
- Screwdriver
- Wrench (optional)

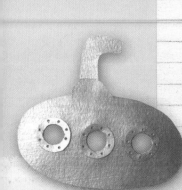

# Instructions:

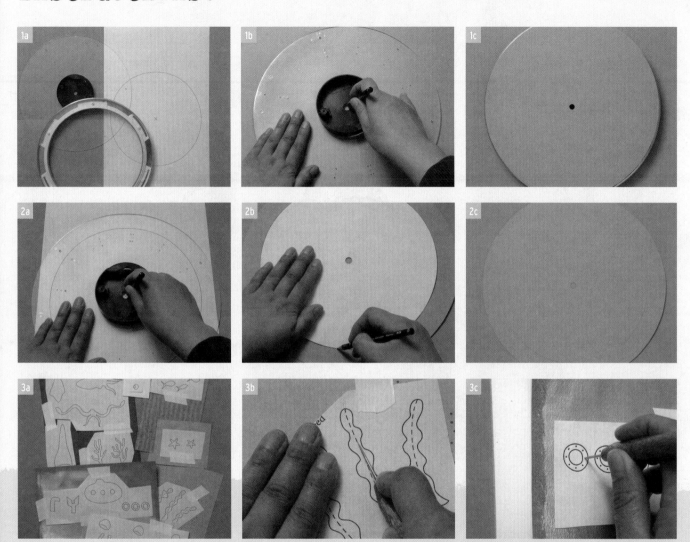

**Tip:** If you are working with children, draw shapes on the paper and have them cut them out with blunt-nosed scissors, rather than cutting the shapes with secured templates.

1 First, dismantle the parts of your clock. Take the clock frame, the clock face, the background template and the paper for the background (1a). Place the clock face on the paper and trace the outline and the central hole with a pencil (1b). Cut the background along the pencil lines, put it in the clock frame and make sure it fits well (1c).

2 Place the clock face on the background template, matching the hole with the X mark, and trace the hole (2a). Remove the clock face then cut the background template along the outline and the hole. Centre the template on the background paper, lining up with the holes (2b) and lightly trace the outline (2c).

3 Take all of the templates and the assigned paper for each one and secure them on the paper with masking tape (3a). On the template for the seaweed, firmly score the middle lines with an awl (3b). Place a piece of foam board under the submarine windows, and poke holes with a sharp tool such as an awl or knitting needle along the dots on the template (3c).

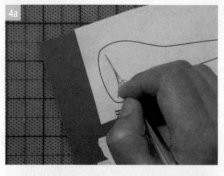

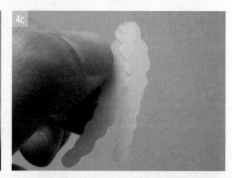

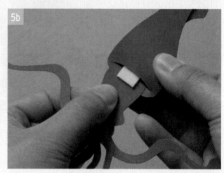

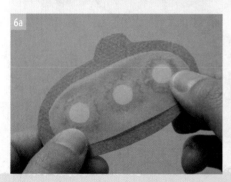

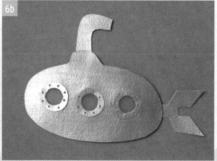

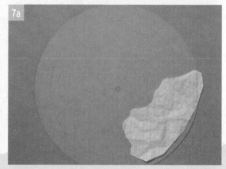

4 With a craft knife, cut the cutting lines inside the sea creatures, submarine and plants first (4a), then cut the outlines. Save the vellum and metallic paper scraps to use later for the submarine windows and bolts. Bend the edges of the seaweed towards you (4b). Glue two arms of jellyfish together (4c), making three sets in all. Bend the arms of the starfish lengthwise all the way to the centre (4d).

5 To assemble the kraken, attach the foreground tentacles to the background tentacles, and the body to the fin, using foam tape (5a). Apply foam tape on the head extension, and slide it through the slot on the body (5b). Position and attach the head to the body. Glue the eye to the head.

6 To assemble the submarine, first glue the window frames to the submarine body, matching the window holes. Cut a piece of vellum smaller than the body but large enough to cover the windows (6a). On the back of the body, thinly apply glue around the holes, and attach the vellum. Attach the propeller and the periscope on the back of the body, using foam tape (6b).

7 Take the background and the paper for the reef. To give the reef a rock-like texture, crumple the paper, then flatten it out again. Repeat this process if necessary until it looks sufficiently crumpled. Cut the paper into the shape of a big rock (7a). To make the leafy texture of the reef, tear one big piece

from the paper to make a base for the reef (7b), then tear the remaining paper into smaller pieces and loosely glue all the torn pieces to the base (7c).

8 Position the reef, seaweed and coral along the pencil line, and glue them to the background (8a). Attach the starfish and fish anywhere you like, using glue or foam tape. On the back of each jellyfish hood, apply glue on the bottom below the cut, and attach the hood to the background. Open up the slot, and slide the jellyfish arms through. Attach the base of the arms to the background behind the hood (8b).

9 Keep all of the pieces as flat as possible. Trim any paper sticking out beyond the edge of the background and erase the pencil lines. Put the clock face in the frame and position the clock hanger pointing up. Mark the location of the top screw hole on the frame (9a). Take the clock face out, and place it straight, face up.

10 Position the seascape on the clock face and assemble the clock parts. Cut the clock hands down in size (10a), leaving just enough surface to attach the kraken and the submarine. Put foam tape on the clock hands, and stick on the kraken and the submarine (10b). Hold the clock face straight up, and turn the clock hands around via the controller at the back of the clock, making sure they can move around the clock face unimpeded. If they can't, gently bend the clock hands or the sculptures as necessary. Assemble the case, matching the marking on the frame with the screw hole on the clock face and put the battery in.

11 On the back of the metallic paper, draw and cut out eight circles small enough to fit on your frame moulding (11a). On the back of the circles, emboss the edges to create the appearance of bolts. Put some foam tape on the back of each bolt, and stick the bolts onto the clock frame an equal distance apart to make the frame look like the porthole of a submarine (11b).

# The owl &
# the pussycat

'The Owl and the Pussycat' is a well-known poem by Edward Lear.

The love story of this odd couple has captivated many people,

and the poem has been illustrated in numerous ways. Paper sculpture

offers its own unique and charming way to illustrate these characters.

This greeting card is a very easy and fun little rainy-day project

that could be made for a special person on Valentine's Day.

# You will need:

## Materials

- 1 photocopy of all templates on pages 154-157, reproduced at 100%
- 1 sheet of cardstock in the colour of your choice, cut to 6 x 10in (15 x 25cm), for the cover
- Several sheets of cardstock in the colours of your choice for the background and the scenery
- Masking tape
- 1 sheet of white cardstock for the insert to make the stars and moon visible
- 1 sheet of unryu paper, at least 8½ x 11in (21.6 x 28cm), the denser the fibre the better, for the owl and the pussycat
- Glue
- Foam tape, ½in (12mm) wide

## Tools

- Cutting mat
- Metal ruler
- Awl
- Craft knife
- Scissors (optional)
- Tweezers
- Spoon-tip wooden burnisher
- Ballpoint pen

# Instructions:

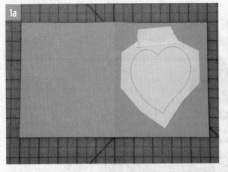

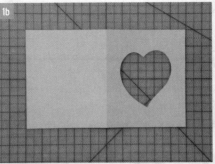

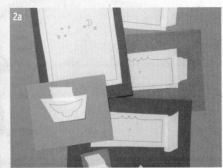

1 Place your cover paper horizontally on your cutting mat. Find the middle, and make a vertical scoreline from top to bottom, using a ruler and an awl, to make the fold of the card. Fold it, then flatten it out again. Place the paper face up so that the crease is raised. Place the heart template centrally on the right half of the paper, securing it with a piece of low-tack masking tape (see page 26) (1a). Cut the heart shape out (1b), then carefully remove the template from the cover.

2 Secure the rest of the templates on each assigned paper (2a). For the background, cut out the stars and the moon first (2b), and then the outline. Cut out all the remaining layers (2c).

3 Take the piece of white cardstock and cut it down to 4½ x 5½in (11 x 14cm). Put it to one side. Then, on the back of a piece of white scrap paper, draw some hearts measuring about ¼-½in (6-12mm) wide (3a) and cut them out.

4 Take the unryu paper and tear off two pieces for the cat and the owl, 1in (2.5cm) longer than the animals in the master template (4a). Using tweezers, tear bits of the paper to create the shape of ears (4b). Position the animals on the master template (4c). If the bottom ends protrude below the boat, tear them off so they fit inside the boat.

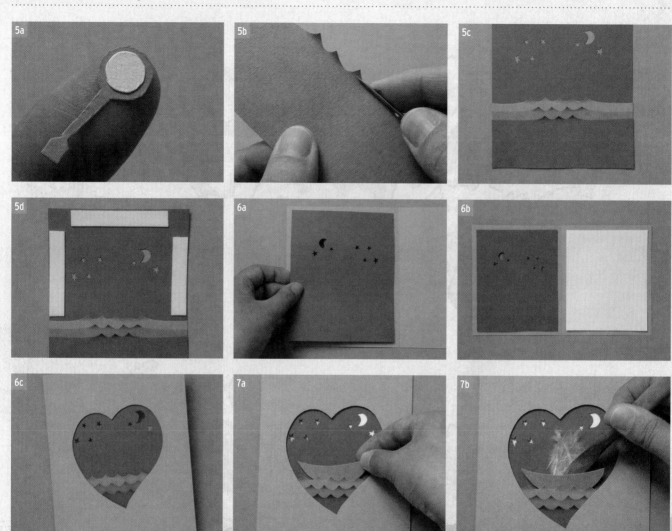

5 Using the guitar parts, centre and glue guitar part B on the round part of guitar part A (5a). Take the waves and the background. Curl the waves towards you (5b) (see page 32). Stack the background and the waves, lining up the bottoms, and glue the pieces to each other (5c). Cut three strips of foam tape and stick them close to the edges of the background paper, but not on the waves (5d).

6 Take the cover and place it face down, so that the heart side is on the back of the left-hand side of the cover. Centre and attach the background to the left side of the cover, face down (6a). Take the white cardstock, centre it and glue it down on the opposite side (6b). Close the cover, and place it face up (6c).

7 Take the boat and the owl body. On the back of the boat, apply glue on the flap. Position the boat behind the waves, so that the flap gets hidden, and attach it to the background (7a). On the back of the owl, put some glue on the bottom. Position the owl behind the boat, using the master template as a reference. Slide a burnisher behind the boat, and burnish the glued area (7b).

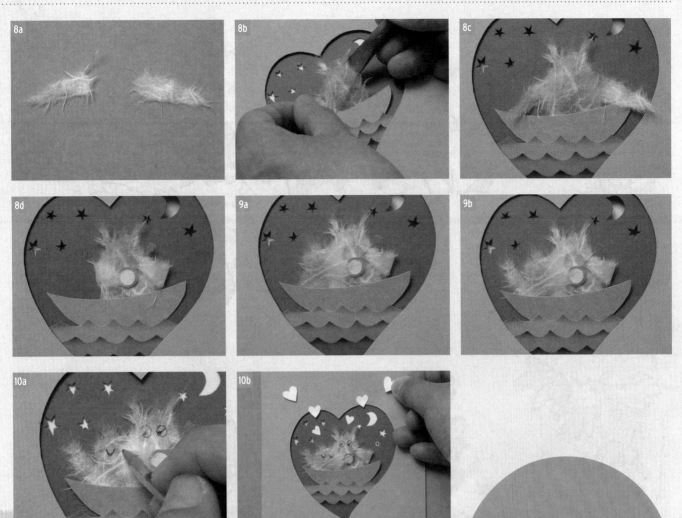

8 Tear two skinny wedges from the unryu paper, about 1in (2.5cm) long, for the wings (8a). On the back of each wing, apply glue to the wider end (8b). Position the glued side of each wing behind each side of the body, and attach the wings to the background paper (8c). Take the guitar and stick it to the owl, using foam tape. Position and glue the wing tips on the guitar (8d).

9 Next to the owl, glue the cat to the background in the same way you did with the owl (9a). Tear a piece of unryu paper for the cat's tail, and glue it to the background behind the cat's body (9b).

10 Lastly, draw eyes on the animals with a ballpoint pen (10a) and attach the heart shapes around the animals (10b).

**Tip:** Using torn pieces of unryu paper works well for making animals, as it creates an impression of fur and feathers. You could adapt this technique to make an animal-themed decor for a child's room.

# Coat of arms

Centuries ago, a coat of arms was used for soldiers to distinguish themselves from their enemies. Since then, people have used coats of arms to represent themselves, their families or their organizations. Each is unique, emblazoned with a collection of meaningful symbols. You can use the basic banner and shield templates from this project as a starting point for your own coat of arms: put your name on the banner and choose symbols that are meaningful to you to decorate the shield.

# You will need:

## Materials

- 1 photocopy of all templates on pages 158-159, enlarged to 300% and alphabet template on pages 160-161 (optional)
- 1 sheet of medium- to heavyweight paper, at least 18 x 24in (46 x 61cm), for the background
- Masking tape
- 2 sheets of cardstock in the colour of your choice for the banner
- 1 sheet of cardstock for each of the colours used for the symbols and the shield, colours of your choice
- 1 sheet of cardstock for the letters in a colour of your choice
- 1 sheet of foam board, 20 x 30 x $\frac{3}{16}$in (50 x 76 x 0.5cm), or bigger than your shield size, for support and embossing
- Double-sided foam tape
- Double-sided tape
- Glue

## Tools

- Craft knife
- Scissors (optional)
- Cutting mat
- Pencil
- Stapler
- Awl
- Stylus
- Metal ruler
- French curve

# Instructions:

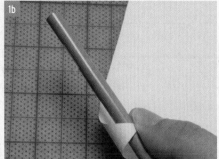

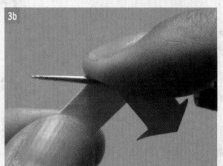

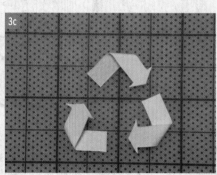

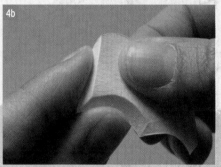

1 With masking tape, secure the master template to the sheet of medium- to heavyweight paper that is to be used for the background (1a). Cut along the outline of the template, then remove the template and put it to one side. Curl the corners of the background paper by rolling them around a pencil (1b).

2 Lay out in front of you the rest of the templates and the assigned papers for each one. With masking tape, secure the shield template to the paper and cut the shield out. For the squares, stack together three sheets of paper in different colours. Place the template on the stack close to the edges, and staple the four layers of paper together (2a). Cut out the squares.

3 Make three layers of paper for the recycling logo and hearts by stacking or folding the paper. With a stapler or masking tape, secure the templates for the arrow, the hearts (3a) and the book on each assigned paper. (Please note that the book will be reversed, so if your paper has different textures on the front and back, make sure you secure the template on the back of the paper.) Cut out the arrows and then fold each arrow over an awl (3b) to make the recycling logo shape (3c).

4 Cut out the hearts, then on the back of each one emboss the edges with a stylus (4a). For the book, firmly score the broken lines with an awl, then cut the outline. Flip the book and gently bend the scored areas away from you (4b). Then, score down the middle of the book spread, and pinch the scored area from behind the book (4c).

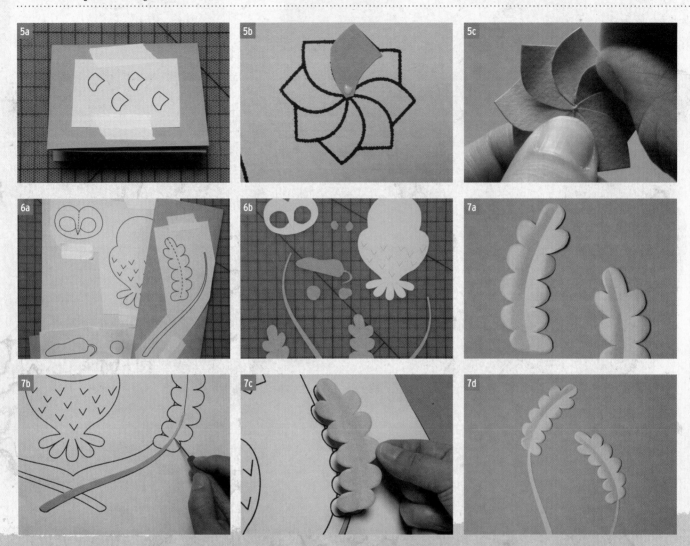

5a
5b
5c
6a
6b
7a
7b
7c
7d

5 Fold the paper for the pinwheel wings in half, then in half again so that you have four layers. Secure the templates on the folded paper (5a) and cut out the shapes; you will have 16 pieces in total. To assemble the first pinwheel (with eight pieces), position one pinwheel wing on the master template and dab some glue on the base of the wing (5b). Position and attach another wing, overlapping with the first wing. Keep on attaching the wings. When the last wing is attached to the previous one, bring the free end to the back of the first wing and glue the wings together (5c). Curl the wings towards you. Then make the second pinwheel using the remaining eight pieces.

6 Fold the paper for the leaves in half then, using masking tape, secure the templates for the leaves, owl parts (head reversed) and the mouse on each assigned paper (6a). Firmly score the broken lines on the owl head and the leaves, using a metal ruler for the straight lines and a French curve for the curved ones. For the owl body, use a craft knife to cut the cutting lines inside the outlines first, then cut the outlines. Now cut out all of the shapes (6b).

7 Place the leaves scored side down, and emboss the edges with a burnisher. Turn them over, and bend the scored lines towards you to make creases. Curl both sides of each leaf (7a). Position one of the stems on the master template (7b) and then glue the corresponding leaf to the stem (7c). Repeat on the other set (7d).

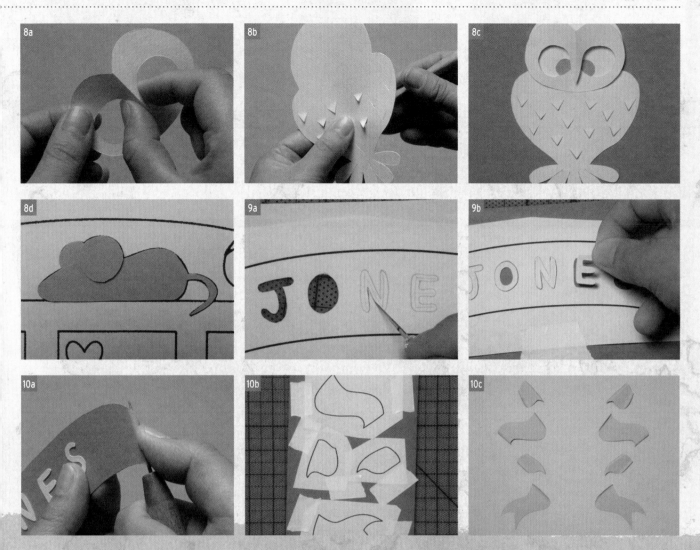

8 Bend the scored area on the owl head (8a). Working from behind the owl body, push the feather patterns out with your fingers or a long tool such as a burnisher or stylus (8b). Bring out the master template and position the owl's body on it. On the back of the owl's head, apply glue to the bottom of the head, and place it down on the body layer, then glue the eyes through the head to the body layer (8c). Now position the mouse's body on the master template. Attach the background ear to the back of the mouse's head and the foreground ear to the front using foam tape (8d).

9 On the banner 1 template, write your required word or name in pencil - you can use the alphabet template. Thicken up the letters by drawing an outline around each letter, about 1/16in (1.5mm) away. With masking tape, secure the banner 1 template to the designated cardstock and cut out the letters (9a). Detach the template and secure it to the paper selected for the banner. Position and glue the cutout letters onto the banner paper (9b).

10 Cut along the outline of banner 1 template then make a tight curl away from you on both ends (10a). Fold another sheet of paper for the banner in half. Secure the other banner templates 2-5 to the folded paper (10b) and cut them out. Curl up the ends where they will meet the upper layers; curl away the ends where they will meet the layers below (10c).

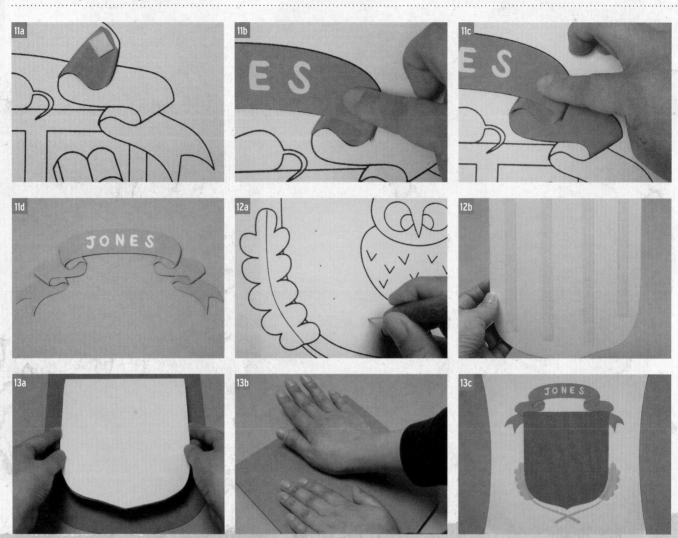

11 Position banner 2 on the master template and put a piece of foam tape on its upper corner (11a). Attach banner 1 to banner 2 (11b). Now position banner 3 on the master template, apply a piece of foam tape, and attach banner 1 and 2 to banner 3 (11c). Position banner 4, and so on. Repeat on the other side (11d).

12 Place a sheet of foam board under the master template. With an awl, poke some holes about 1in (2.5cm) inside from the shield outline (12a). Put the template to one side. Cut the foam board along the markings to make a support for the shield. Put strips of double-sided tape on top of the support (12b).

13 Carefully, take the shield while keeping the banner and leaves in place and put it face down on your work surface. Centre and attach the support on the shield (13a). Flip the shield over, and burnish the taped areas with your hand (13b). Arrange the banner, shield and the leaves on the background, using the master template as a reference (13c). Take the shield, and put strips of double-sided tape on the support. Attach the shield to the background (13d).

14 Put a few pieces of foam tape on the back of the squares, the pinwheels and the owl (14a). Keep the backing paper on the foam tape for the moment. Attach the recycle logo, the hearts and the book on the squares with foam tape (14b). Arrange the different elements on the shield, using the master template as a reference. When you are happy with the arrangement, peel off the backing paper from the foam tape, position the pieces, and press each one firmly down (14c).

15 Cut a piece of foam-board smaller than banner 1 to make a support and put it on the back of the banner (15a). Apply double-sided tape to the support. Position and attach the banner to the background above the shield (15b). Attach foam-board supports to the backs of the leaves and foam tape to the stems (15c), and put them in place. Now attach the mouse to the background with a foam-board support (15d).

16 To display your paper artwork, make two pieces of looped masking tape (see page 43), and put them on the top two corners on the back of your coat of arms. Position it on the wall (16a). When you are sure you are happy with its location, secure it with more looped masking tape.

# Architectural ornament

This is a versatile project; you can use the ornament to decorate a door, a window or a mirror. If you want to adjust the design to suit your taste, take inspiration from sources such as the exteriors of old buildings or antique furniture and ornaments. When you find something you like, translate it into your own design, using the techniques set out in this project.

# You will need:

## Materials

- 1 photocopy of all the templates on pages 160-161, enlarged to 450%
- 2 sheets of white medium paper, 22 x 30in (56 x 76cm)
- Masking tape
- 1 sheet of foam board, 20 x 30 x $^3/_{16}$in (50 x 76 x 0.5cm), for embossing
- Glue
- Foam tape

## Tools

- Craft knife
- Scissors (optional)
- Cutting mat
- Awl
- French curve
- Spoon-tip wooden burnisher
- Ruler
- Stylus

# Instructions:

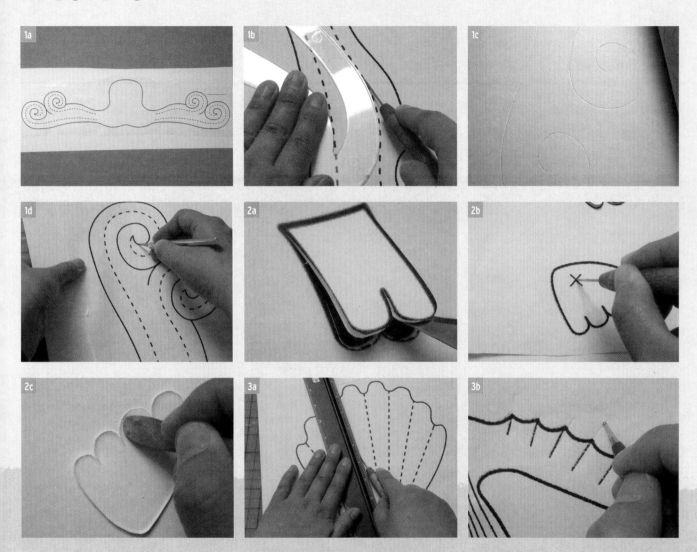

1 Take one of the two sheets of paper for the ornament and cut it in half lengthwise. Secure one side of the waves template to the cut paper with masking tape (1a). Using the cutting mat, firmly score the broken lines on the waves with an awl, using a French curve for guidance (1b). Lift the template and check that the paper is scored (1c). Secure the template with more masking tape if necessary and cut along the outline using a craft knife or scissors (1d).

2 Fold the other piece of cut paper in half and, using masking tape, affix to it the fish templates. Cut along the scalloped sides of the scales, but leave the straight sides uncut (2a). Poke a little hole on the fish head to mark the position of the eyes (2b). Cut out the heads and the eyes. On the back of each head, emboss the edges with a burnisher (2c).

3 Take the second piece of paper and secure one side of the shell and the fish tail and fin templates on it. Score the broken lines on the shell, using a ruler for guidance (3a). Place a sheet of foam board under the paper and firmly trace the patterns on the fish tails and fins with a stylus (3b). Lift the template and emboss the pressed markings. Secure the templates with more tape if necessary, and cut out the shapes of the shell, fish tail and fin.

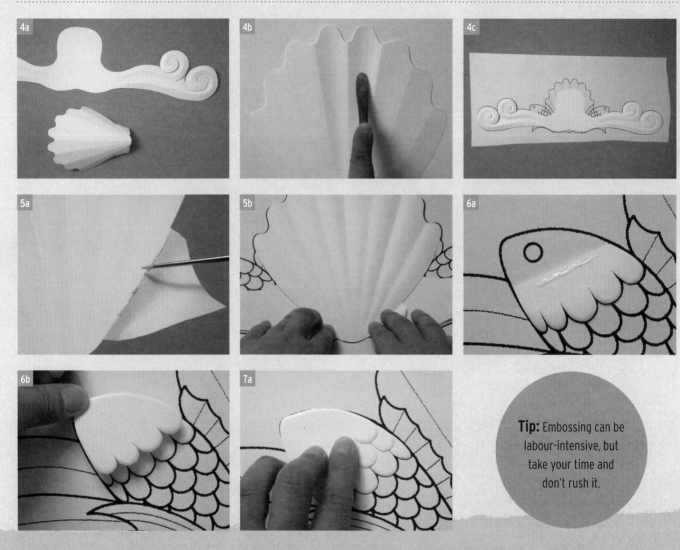

**Tip:** Embossing can be labour-intensive, but take your time and don't rush it.

**4** Place the waves and the shell scored side down. Bend the scored areas away so that raised creases appear (4a). On the waves, score in between the creases, and bend the waves up along the scored lines. Next, emboss the shell by burnishing the paper with pressure in between the creases using a spoon-tip wooden burnisher (4b) and make a wavy curl in each shell wing (see page 32). Take the master template and position the waves on it (4c).

**5** On the back of the shell, apply glue on the raised creases adjacent to each shell wing (5a). Position and press the glued areas down (5b). Take all of the fish layers and divide them into two sets, arranging them in a mirror image. Place the fish tails and fins with the raised surface up.

**6** Cut the bases of the scales for layer 1 and place them on each set. Emboss the scalloped edges on the back. Position scale 1 from one set on the master template, matching the guideline. Apply glue on the straight edge (6a). Attach the head to scale 1 (6b). Put aside and repeat on the other set.

**7** Cut and emboss the scales for layer 2 and position one of the two pieces on the template. Glue the head and scale 1 that you assembled in step 6 to scale 2 (7a). Repeat on the other set. Put them aside, and repeat the process for the other scales.

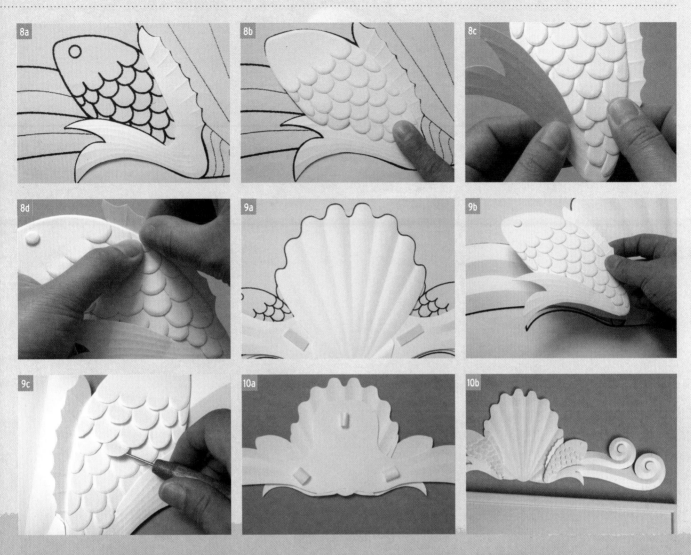

8a 8b 8c 8d 9a 9b 9c 10a 10b

8 Position the fin and the tail from one set on the master template (8a). Apply glue on the area of it that will not be visible when assembled, and press the fish body down (8b). Bring the tail to the front (8c). Next, attach the eye to the marking on the head, using a piece of foam tape, and bend the fin towards you (8d). Repeat on the other fish.

9 Place the waves on the master template and put a few layers of foam tape on each side of the shell (9a). Now position and attach both fish (9b). Slide an awl underneath the scales to gently separate and lift them up (9c).

10 To finish, on the back of the shell, apply a few pieces of looped masking tape (see page 43) (10a). Position the ornament in the designated space (10b). When you are happy with its location, secure it with more looped masking tape, and if necessary, reshape any flattened areas.

# Trumpet flowers

Flowers are an inspiring subject for paper sculpture.
Not only are they beautiful, but the delicate petals and
leaves translate well in paper. Flowers can be complicated
to make because of their complex structures and textures.
However, trumpet flowers have a relatively simple shape,
and the various clusters of tubular, round and pointed shapes
create interesting contrasts. This project also shows you
a simple way to frame a paper sculpture.

# You will need:

## Materials

- 1 photocopy of all the templates on pages 164–166, reproduced at 100%
- Embossing map, for reference (see pages 167–168)
- 1 wooden frame with grooves and swing braces, 8 x 10in (20 x 25cm) with a groove at rabbet depth of about 1in (2.5cm), glass or acrylic included, in the colour of your choice
- Sawtooth hanger
- 1 sheet of mat board, cut to 8 x 10in (20 x 25cm), in the colour of your choice, for the backboard
- 1 sheet of orange cardstock for the flowers and buds
- 1 sheet of reddish-orange cardstock for the flower parts
- 1 sheet of yellow cardstock for the flower parts
- 1 sheet of green cardstock for the leaves
- Masking tape, 1in (2.5cm) wide
- Glue
- 1 sheet of foam board with $\frac{3}{16}$in (5mm) thickness, a little longer than your frame for spacers, plus more for embossing
- 1 pre-cut mount, 8 x 10in (20 x 25cm) with an opening of around $6\frac{1}{2}$ x $4\frac{1}{2}$in (16.5 x 11cm), in the colour of your choice

## Tools

- Blanket
- Metal ruler
- Pencil
- Hammer
- Craft knife
- Scissors (optional)
- Cutting mat
- Spoon-tip wooden burnisher
- Stylus
- Awl

# Instructions:

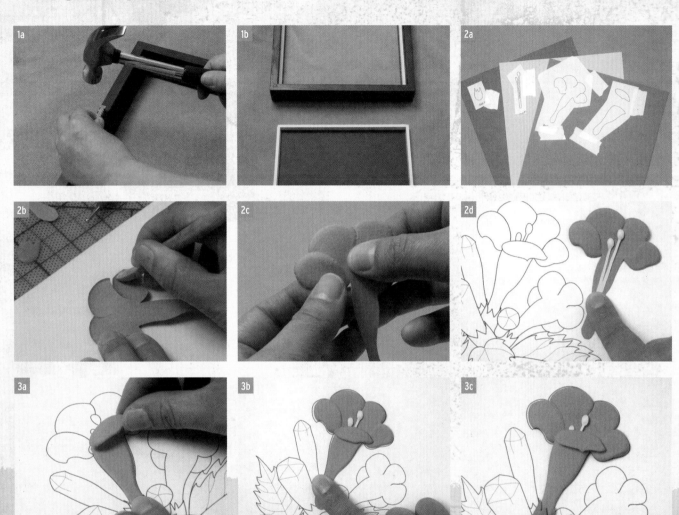

1 Place a blanket on your work surface. Take the glass out of the frame, and put the frame face down on the blanket. Measure the top moulding, find the midpoint, and mark it. Centre the sawtooth hanger on the mark and hammer it down (1a). Using the foam board, prepare your frame with ³⁄₈in (9.5mm) wide frame spacers (see page 38), and prepare the backboard with ¹⁄₂in (12mm) wide mat spacers (1b).

2 Take the master template, flower 1 templates and the colour papers that will make up the flower. Secure the templates on each corresponding paper with masking tape (2a) and then cut out the shapes. Emboss each shape on the back (2b), as shown on page 167. Slightly overlap the background petals (2c). Using the master template, position and glue flower part 1 on the lower part of the background petals (2d).

3 Glue a small looped support to the back of the foreground petal (see page 34). Position the tube on the master template, and attach the petal to the top of the tube (3a). Put them aside. Position the background petals on the template, and apply some glue on the lower half. Attach the tube to the lower part of the background petals (3b). Glue flower part 2 to the bottom of the tube with a small looped support (3c).

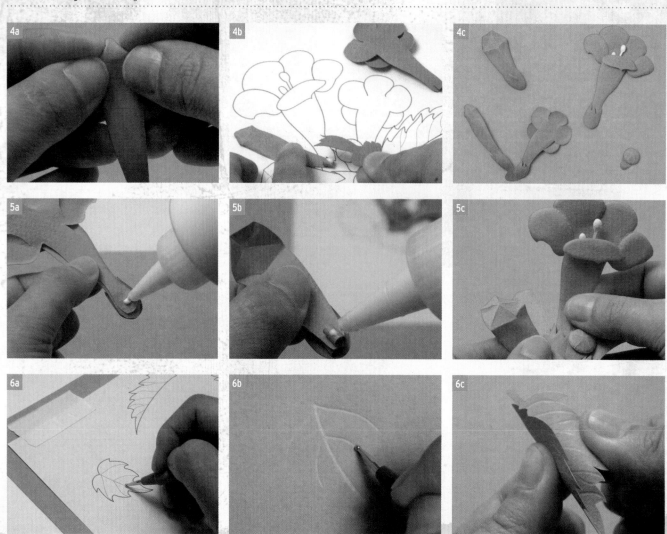

4 Cut out all the parts of flower 2 and bud 3 and place them on a piece of foam board. With a burnisher, deboss the middle of each petal on the front, and emboss the edges of the tube, the flower part 3, and bud 3 on the back. With a stylus, emboss the embossing pattern on top of bud 3 as shown on page 168, then turn it over and bend the embossed lines (4a). Assemble the flower and the bud using small looped supports (4b). Cut, shape and assemble the rest of the buds and flower parts (4c).

5 Position flower 2 and bud 3 on the master template. Attach flower 1 to flower part 3 directly without a small looped support (5a). Position and attach the rest of the buds with small looped supports (5b). Slightly bend flower 1 and bud 1 towards you (5c).

6 Take the templates and the paper for the leaves. Secure one side of the leaf templates onto the paper with masking tape, and place the paper on a piece of foam board. Note that the foreground leaf template is reversed for embossing. Firmly trace the rib lines of the leaves with a stylus (6a). Lift off the template, and re-burnish the pressed marks to emboss the foreground leaf of leaf 2 and deboss leaves 1 and 3 (6b). Put the template back down, and cut the leaves out. On leaves 1 and 3, pinch the middle ribs from behind, and curl both sides of the rib with your fingers (6c).

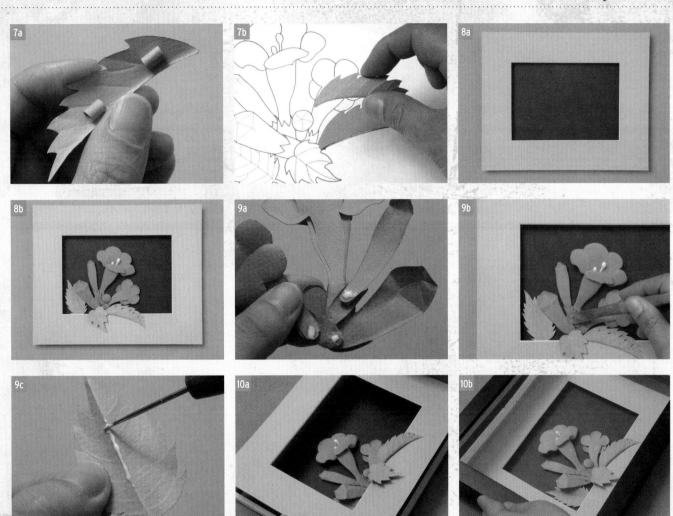

**7** Curl the bottom edge of the foreground leaf of leaf 2 around an awl. On the back, attach a couple of small looped supports (7a). Position the background leaf on the master template and attach the foreground leaf to the background leaf (7b).

**8** Place the mount over the mat spacers (8a). Using the master template as a reference, arrange the flowers and the leaves on the backboard and the mount. Attach leaf 1 to the mount with a small looped support and glue leaf 2 directly onto the mount, without a support (8b).

**9** Carefully, lift the flowers and buds while keeping the mount and leaf 3 in place, and apply some glue on the back (9a). Position the flowers and buds on the backboard, and hold them in place with a long tool, such as a burnisher, until the glue sets (9b). Keeping the mount in place, lift leaf 3 and apply glue on the back along the middle rib (9c). Place the leaf down on the backboard.

**10** Put a blanket on your work surface and place the artwork on it (10a). Position the frame over the sculpture, and carefully place it down (10b). Hold the frame and your artwork altogether, and flip them over. Finally, put the back panel in place, and secure the swing braces to the grooves.

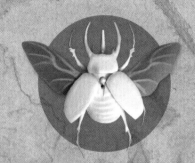

# Beetle specimen

Here you will learn how to make and use an embossing stencil, which is a great way to produce multiple pieces. Taking these instructions as a starting point, you could make a series of beetles, using different colours, or the same body with varying wing or head shapes. The containers used for display are not expensive. I've suggested adding magnetic tape to turn the project into a fridge magnet, so you can make this as a gift that is both decorative and functional.

# You will need:

## Materials

- 1 photocopy of all the templates on page 169, sized to fit in your container
- 1 clear-top metal container, at least 2³⁄₄in (7cm) in diameter and 1in (2.5cm) deep
- 1 sheet of foam board, at least 8¹⁄₂ x 11 x ³⁄₁₆in (21.6 x 28 x 0.5cm), for supports and embossing
- 1 sheet of white cardstock for the body
- Glue
- 2 sheets of heavy cardstock, in any colour, for the background and the embossing stencil
- Double-sided tape
- Magnetic tape
- Masking tape
- 1 sheet of white vellum, 8¹⁄₂ x 11in (21.6 x 28cm), or A4 size, for the wings
- 1 sheet of white tissue paper, 8¹⁄₂ x 11in (21.6 x 28cm), for the legs and antennae
- Foam tape
- 1 dressmaker's pin, cut down if necessary to fit in your container

## Tools

- Cutting mat
- Craft knife
- Pencil
- Lightbox (optional) for tracing the embossing stencil
- Stylus
- Tweezers

**Tip:** A window in daylight makes an effective substitute for a lightbox.

# Instructions:

1 Cut a circle out of foam board about 1in (2.5cm) smaller than your display container (1a). Trace the bottom of the container on one of the sheets of heavy cardstock and cut it out. Make sure it fits inside your container. Put glue in the middle of the foam-board piece and attach it to the background paper (1b). Put a couple of pieces of double-sided tape on the bottom of the foam piece, and stick it inside the container (1c). Attach two strips of magnetic tape to the back of the container (1d).

2 Take the lower abdomen template and the remaining sheet of heavy cardstock. Secure the template to the cardstock with a couple of pieces of masking tape. Carefully cut out the shape to make an embossing stencil. It is important that the stencil has a clean cut, so make sure your blade is sharp. Remove the template (2a).

3 Place the stencil over a light source, facing down. Secure the paper for the lower abdomen on the stencil, also facing down. Trace all around the edge of the stencil with a stylus (3a). Move the paper straight down by about $\frac{1}{16}$in (1.5mm) (3b). Trace only on the bottom part.

4 Lower the paper by another $\frac{1}{16}$in (1.5mm) and again trace only the bottom part. Repeat until the shape has five segments (4a). When all the segments are embossed, turn the paper to the front. Carefully cut out the whole embossed shape - not each segment - right below the embossed surface. Curve the abdomen lengthways using your fingers (4b).

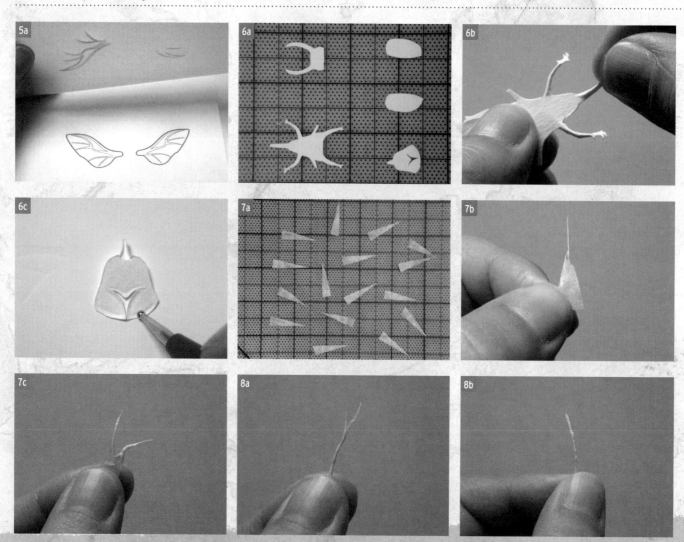

5 Take the inner wing templates and the vellum, and secure the vellum to the template with a piece of tape. Place the templates and the vellum on a sheet of foam board. Using a stylus, emboss the vellum, following the wing pattern. Lift the vellum to check the patterns are fully embossed (5a). Remove the foam sheet and cut the wings along the outline.

6 Secure the rest of the templates on the cardstock and cut out all the pieces (6a). Using a stylus, emboss the head and legs layer where indicated on the template on page 169. Squeeze the legs and horn with your fingers and a pair of tweezers to make them more slender and cylindrical (6b). Emboss the thorax, upper abdomen (6c) and the outer wings.

7 Take the sheet of tissue paper and fold it in half three times to make eight layers. Cut two triangles from it, about ¼in (6mm) wide on the bottom and 1in (2.5cm) long, so you end up with 16 triangles (although you will only use 14 - keep the other two as spares) (7a). Roll each triangle lengthwise from the tip to halfway down (7b). Put glue on one of the pieces, and attach it to another piece at the base so they overlap (7c).

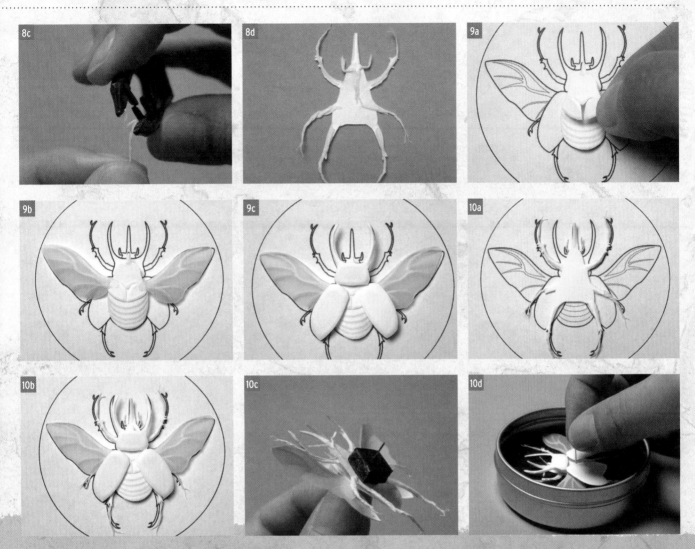

8 Twist the pieces together from the wider ends, leaving a split at the end to make the beetle's claws (8a). Make five more sets, so you have six claws altogether. Roll up the remaining two triangles to make two antennae (8b) and bend the wider tips with a pair of tweezers (8c). Now glue the claws and the antennae to the back of the head and legs layer (8d), using the master template as a reference.

9 Take the master template and the lower and upper abdomen. Position the lower abdomen on the master template, and glue the upper abdomen to the lower abdomen (9a). Apply glue to the back of the inner wing bases, and attach them to the upper abdomen (9b). Put a piece of foam tape on the back of the thorax and the outer wings, and attach the pieces to the upper abdomen (9c).

10 Put these pieces aside and position the head and legs layer on the master template (10a). Attach the other parts of the body to the head and legs with foam tape (10b). Cut a small piece out of foam board. Place it on the back of the beetle, and pin them together (10c), and then pin the beetle to the background (10d). If the dressmaker's pin has been cut down to fit in the container, use an awl to poke a hole in the middle of the upper abdomen and the foam piece.

# Cameo

A traditional cameo is a relief carving, usually featuring a
subject in white set against a colour background. The subjects
vary, but profile portraits are common. The style is classical,
elegant, smooth and lifelike. Cameo carving requires a high
degree of skill, but you can mimic the look with paper sculpture
to create a portrait of a loved one. If you lack confidence in
your drawing skills, use a tracing of a photograph to create
the master template. To display the finished artwork,
I've used a non-traditional frame: an old clock case.

# You will need:

## Materials

- Embossing map template example (see page 170)
- Photograph of a profile shot that is large enough to trace
- 1 table clock with the clock parts removed
- 1 clock face, for framing
- Tracing paper
- Sheet of clear overlay film, big enough to cover your photo
- 1 sheet of coloured paper larger than your clock face for the background to the cameo
- A few sheets of white medium-weight paper large enough for your cameo
- Masking tape
- 1 sheet of foam board, 8½ x 11in (21.6 x 28cm) for embossing
- Glue
- Screws from the clock for reassembling it

## Tools

- Permanent marker
- Dry-erase board cleaner
- Cotton buds
- Paper towel
- Pencil
- Ruler
- Craft knife
- Scissors (optional)
- Cutting mat
- Stylus
- Spoon-tip wooden burnisher
- Awl
- Tweezers
- Screwdriver

# Instructions:

1 Trace your photo, following the instructions on page 24. Trace the main elements such as the neck, hair, head, basic facial features, jawline, and any wrinkles or facial hair (1a). Then trace other elements such as spectacles. Simplify the hairstyle.

2 Measure the diameter of your clock window, then prepare a master template like the one on page 170 by making a photocopy on the film, adjusting the size to fit into your clock window. Secure a sheet of tracing paper to your master template with a piece of masking tape (2a).

3 Trace the neck and the outline of your clock window. Extend the neck long enough to be overlapped with the head and hair (3a). If the neck is covered by hair or clothing, draw estimated lines to complete the layer. Move or replace the tracing paper to lay a clean area over the template.

4 Trace the outline of the face, eye opening, nostril, lips, jawline and ear. Include elements such as wrinkles or moles. Complete the layer with an extension line on the opposite side of the face, and leave enough room to attach the hair (4a).

5 Separate the hair, eyebrow and eyelid. If the hair has layers, allow room to overlap it with other layers (5a). Separate two layers for the eye: one for the whole eyeball, and one without the iris (5b). Separate accessories or facial hair (5c).

6 Place the clock face on each piece of paper for the figure and background, and trace the outline. Cut the background to fit in the clock frame. On the white paper, centre the neck tracing within the outline of the clock face; extend the neckline to the clock-face outline (6a). Cut out the neck outline only (6b).

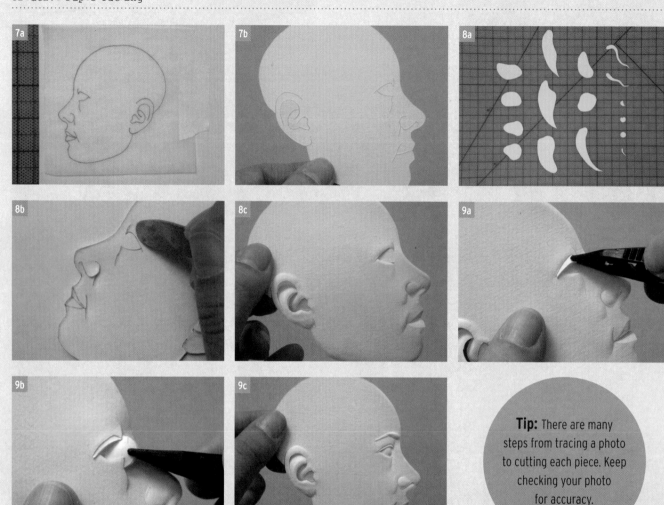

**Tip:** There are many steps from tracing a photo to cutting each piece. Keep checking your photo for accuracy.

**7** Take another piece of white paper and your tracing of the head. Secure the tracing on the back of the paper with a piece of masking tape, tracing side down (7a). Burnish the lip outline onto the paper with a stylus. Lift the tracing paper to check that the line has transferred properly. Cut the cutting lines inside the outline, all except for the lip outline. Then cut the template outline. (7b).

**8** Secure the rest of the tracings, facing up, on the front of the paper and cut out the shapes (8a). On the back of the head, emboss the cut edges, using the embossing map on page 170 as a reference. Use a spoon-tip wooden burnisher for the large areas (8b) and a stylus for small areas. Score the lip lines with an awl. Turn the head over, and bend the lip lines away till the raised creases appear. Pull the ear lobe out towards you (8c).

**9** Referring to your master template or photograph, position the eyelid through the eye opening (9a) and glue it to the head from behind. Glue the eye layers together. Emboss the eye on the back. Cut a tiny strip out of scrap paper and make a looped support (see page 34), small enough to be hidden behind the eye. Attach it to the back of the eye. Position the eye on the head. Put glue on the support and attach it to the head (9b). Emboss the eyebrow on the back and glue it to the head (9c).

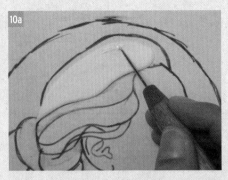
10a

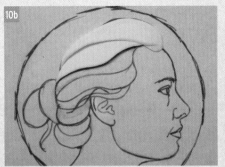
10b

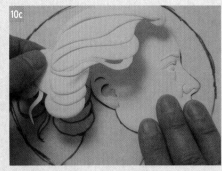
10c

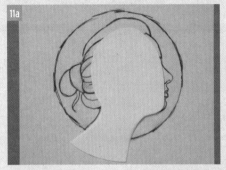
11a

11b

11c

12a

12b

**10** To make the hair as shown in this example, place each layer of the hair on the master template to see where it will be visible when assembled. Turn over the layer, and emboss the visible edges. Start gluing layer by layer, without a support (10a, 10b). Position the head on the master template (10c) and glue the assembled hair to the head, matching the guidelines. If your subject has a beard, shape, assemble and attach this to the face, too.

**11** Now take the neck piece and emboss the edges on both sides of the neck. Position it on the master template (11a). Affix a looped support to the back of the head and apply glue (11b). Attach the headpiece to the neck piece (11c).

**12** Put a dab of glue on the back of the head, then take the background, line the bottom of the neck with the background edge, and gently hold the glued area down until the glue sets (12a). Shape any spectacles or accessories and attach them to the figure. Finally, put the cameo and clock face in the clock case, and finish assembling (12b).

# Dog portrait

Portraits make great subjects for paper sculpture because the art form creates a sense of tangibility. This is a fun project for dog lovers. You will learn how to create an impression of a dog's furry coat using simple, stylized jagged, curvy or wavy cuts and very few layers. The techniques used in this project can also be adapted for other animals such as cats, wolves, rabbits, bears and koalas. As with the previous project, here we use an upcycled wall-clock case as an alternative to the traditional picture frame.

# You will need:

## Materials

- Photograph of a dog, large enough to trace
- Embossing map and guidelines for separating layers, for reference (see pages 171-176)
- 1 clock case with the clock parts removed, and centre marked (see page 41)
- 1 clock face centre marked, with the hanger still attached, for framing and hanging (see page 41)
- 1 sheet of clear overlay film, big enough to cover your photo
- Tracing paper
- Masking tape
- A few sheets of coloured medium-weight paper in the shades of your dog's coat, larger than your frame, for the portrait background and the dog portrait
- 1 sheet of foam board, 8½ x 11in (21.6 x 28cm), for embossing
- Glue
- Screws from the clock

## Tools

- Permanent marker
- Dry-erase board cleaner
- Cotton buds
- Paper towel
- Pencil
- Ruler
- Craft knife
- Cutting mat
- Spoon-tip wooden burnisher
- Stylus
- Awl
- Screwdriver

**Tip:** Make your own custom-coloured paper to use for dogs with patterned coats.

# Instructions:

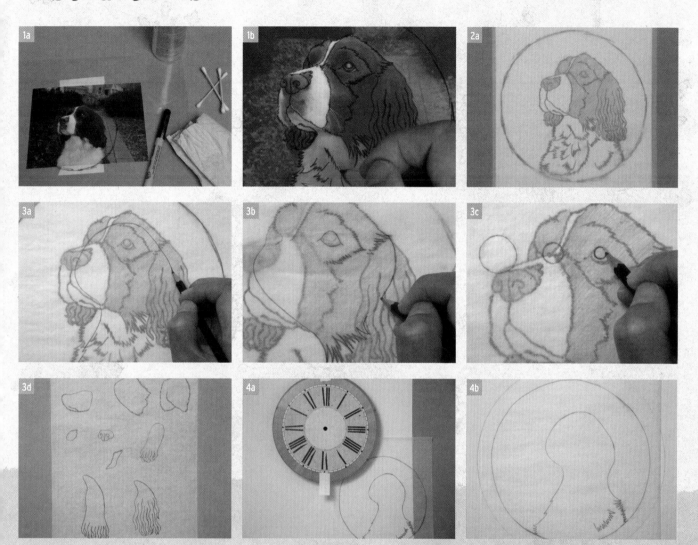

Prepare your photograph and a sheet of clear overlay film as described on page 24 (1a). Within the shape of your clock window, use the marker to trace the dog's major features such as the neck, head, muzzle, mouth, eyes, nose, ears and spots. Separate any furry parts into two or more layers. Try using jagged, curvy or wavy lines to stylize fur patterns (1b).

Remove the photo and measure the diameter of your clock window. Make a copy of the film to create a master template, reducing or enlarging the tracing according to the size of your clock window. If your dog has spots on its coat, mark the colour of these on the master template. Secure a sheet of tracing paper to your master template with a piece of masking tape (2a).

Create separate layers, as shown in the examples on pages 173-176. Each time, move or replace the tracing paper to lay a clean area over the template. First, separate the neck and the outline of your clock window (3a). Make extra room above the neck to attach the head later. Create additional layers for a furry neck. Next, create layers for the head (3b). Extend the lines to complete the shapes of the features. Create layers for each eye (3c). Create layers for the muzzle, nose, ears and any spots on the coat (3d).

Take the clock face, the neck template and the paper for the neck (4a). Put the clock face on the paper and make two tracings of the outline. Cut one of them to make the backing paper, and on the other tracing, centre the neck template within the transparent outline of the clock face

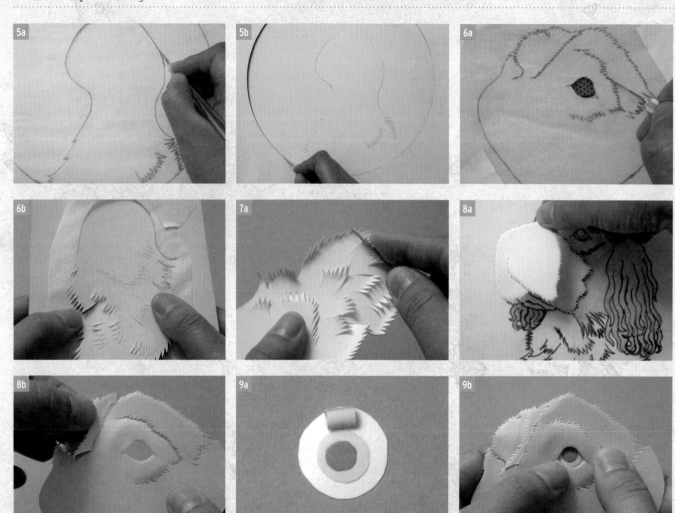

(4b).

5 Secure the template to the paper with masking tape. Cut out all around the neck, except at the bottom where you have the outline of the clock window (5a). Remove the template, then cut the traced outline (5b). Put each cut paper in the clock case, making sure they fit well. Secure the rest of the templates on the corresponding papers.

6 Cut any cutting lines inside the outlines before cutting the outline (6a). Check the back to see that all the lines have been cut through. Cut the jagged patterns from the inside corners. When all of the cuts have been made, push the cut paper and wiggle it a few times to pop out the shape (6b).

7 After the shapes have been cut, emboss the paper on the back, referring to the embossing map on page 170. Use a spoon-tip burnisher for the larger areas and a stylus for smaller areas. With an awl, curl the longer fur patterns away or towards you depending on the nature of the dog's coat (7a).

8 Turn your attention to the features that consist of multiple layers. Position the second-to-top layer on the master template, then glue the top layer to it, matching the guidelines without supports (8a). Repeat if you have more layers. Insert any spots through slots, and directly glue them from the back (8b).

9 To assemble the eye(s), first glue the pupil directly to the iris. Then glue the iris to the eyeball. (You can skip this eyeball layer if your photo shows only the iris and pupil.) Now emboss the eye from the back. Put a looped support (see page 34) on the extended area of the eye(s) (9a). Position and attach the eye(s) to the head from behind (9b).

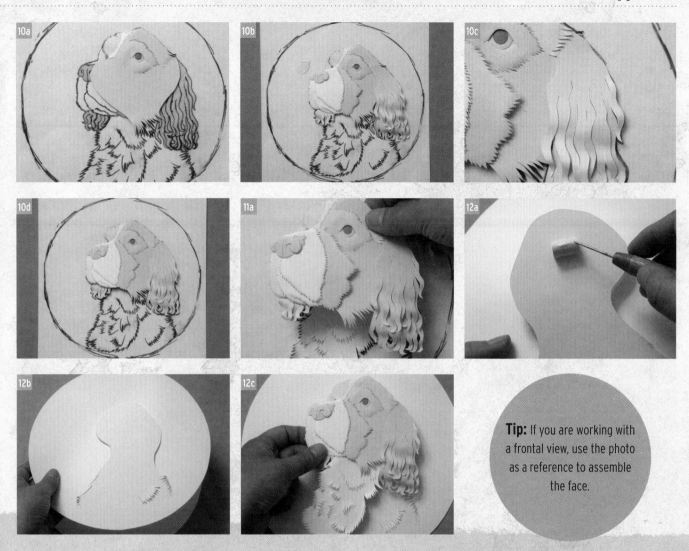

**Tip:** If you are working with a frontal view, use the photo as a reference to assemble the face.

10 Take the master template and place the head on it (10a). Lay out the facial features on the head (10b). Attach the nose to the muzzle with a looped support, and attach the muzzle to the head without a support. Check whether each ear goes behind or in front of the head and attach it accordingly (10c, 10d).

11 Put a looped support on the foremost neck layer and apply glue to it. Position the layer on the master template (11a). (Skip this step if your piece does not have an additional layer for the neck.) Position the head and place it down.

12 Take the neck base and the backing paper. Attach a looped support on the back of the neck and dab glue on it (12a). Attach the neck base to the backing paper, matching the outlines (12b). Using the master template as a reference, position and glue the head to the neck base (12c). Finally, follow the steps from step 2 (2b) onwards on page 41 and finish framing the piece.

# Graffiti

Graffiti, or street art, is a popular and vibrant art form.
Now you can create a piece of 3D paper graffiti, using your walls
as a canvas. While many of the projects in this book have fixed
designs for you to follow quite closely, this project
encourages you to be more creative. Make several random
objects, or choose a theme, and put them together on the wall
any way you like. Start small, then add pieces to expand your
graffiti as your creative inspiration strikes!

# You will need:

## Materials

- Alphabet template on page 177 or copy paper to create your own letters
- Starburst template on page 178 (optional)
- Phone book or newspaper stack to place under paper when drawing letters
- Several sheets of medium-weight paper, 22 x 28in (56 x 71cm) in neon colours
- Masking tape
- Glue
- Foam board, cut into a couple of strips 10 x $\frac{3}{16}$ x $\frac{1}{2}$in (25cm x 5mm x 12mm)
- Foam tape
- Removable adhesive (optional), see page 15

## Tools

- Solid graphite
- Pencil
- Awl
- French curve (optional)
- Cutting mat
- Craft knife
- Scissors (optional)

# Instructions:

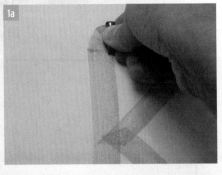

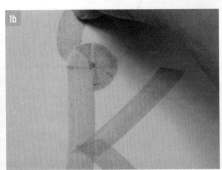

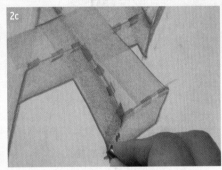

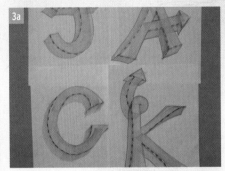

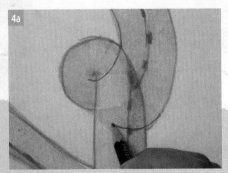

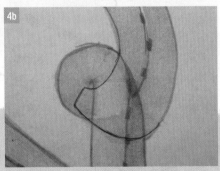

1 Write your letters on copy paper (see steps 1–2 on page 23). To embellish a letter like the 'K' here, place the solid graphite where you need to make a loop. Pivot the graphite in an arc as far as you can (1a). Reposition, and pivot to finish the loop. Stop at the vertical line and draw the arrow outside (1b).

2 Define the letter edges with strong outlines (2a). To add dimension, mark the left and bottom edges on each letter with thick broken lines. Put the graphite next to the lines at 45 degrees. Follow the lines, keeping the same angle

(2b). Define the left and bottom edges of the sides; ignore shades that overlap with the letter surface. Mark outside corners with thick broken lines (2c).

3 Create layers as needed. Here, the arrow overlaps the main part of the letter K, making two layers (3a). Photocopy the letters, reversed, adjusting the scale. Make one copy per layer. Make one unreversed copy for letters to be assembled.

4 To separate the K, draw estimated outlines for the hidden area of the loop on one of the

templates, starting from the arrow (4a). Extend the lines to overlap with the visible part of the loop and close up the arrow shape. Darken the extended outline to define the cutting line (4b).

5 With masking tape, stick one side of each template on the back of the letter paper. On the template, score the broken lines with an awl. Use a French curve for guidance. Cut any cutting lines inside the outlines. Lift the templates to check that all the lines are cut and scored. Cut out the letters; turn to the right side (5a).

6 Gently bend the paper along the scored lines away from you to make raised creases (6a). Locate any inside corners and score them on the front of the paper. Bend the scored part of the paper towards you (6b). Assemble any letters that have more than one layer with some glue, using the extra copy as a guide (6c).

7 Take the foam-board strip and some foam tape. Cover the strip with foam tape on both sides to make a foam-board support. Keep the backing paper on the foam tape for the moment. Arrange all the letters on your work surface so they overlap each other a little (7a). Cut the foam-board support and stick it to the back of the foremost letter where it overlaps with the adjacent letter. Position the letter and press it down (7b). Repeat this process for the rest of the letters (7c).

8 Once all the letters are attached to each other, place the sheet of paper for the letter background face down. If you have a long word, glue a few sheets of letter background paper together before putting the letters on. Turn the letters over and place them on the paper (8a). Draw an outline to make a frame from the letters (8b). Stylize the outline if you wish. Put the letters aside and cut out the background for the letters (8c).

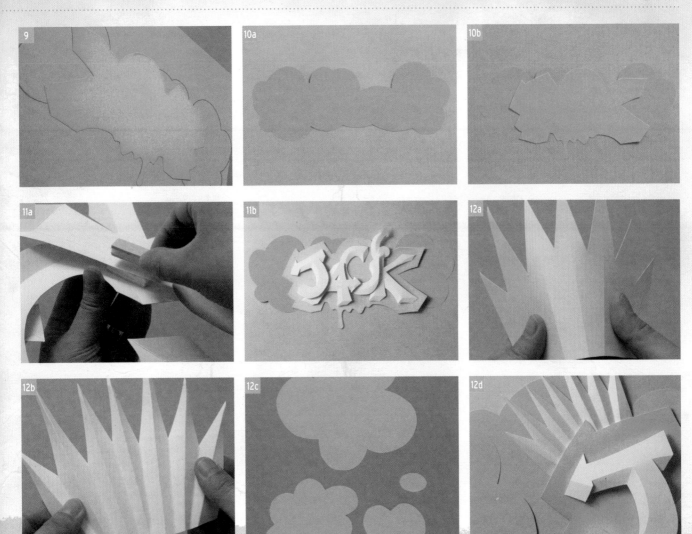

9 Place the paper to be used for the cloud background face down and put the letter background on the paper, face down. Draw cloud shapes around the letter background (9), then remove the letter background. Close the cloud shape by connecting the broken lines, leaving room to attach the letter background. Cut out the shape.

10 Put a few pieces of looped masking tape (see page 43) on the back of the cloud, close to the edges. Lightly attach the cloud to the wall (don't worry about making it level for the moment) (10a). Make a few more pieces of looped tape and put them on the back of the letter background. Attach the letter background to the cloud shape (10b).

11 On the back of the letters, attach some foam-board supports to the supported spots (11a). Position the letters onto the letter background, and press the taped areas down (11b). After all the layers have been arranged, straighten up the paper if necessary (see page 43). Secure the letter background to the cloud background with some glue or foam tape and then the cloud background to the wall with more looped tape or removable adhesive. If your graffiti is long and heavy, attach the letter background to the clouds with some glue or foam tape, and attach the cloud background to the wall with removable adhesive.

12 Make and add more elements as desired. To make the starburst, secure the template from page 178 to the assigned paper. Score the broken lines on the starburst using a ruler and an awl and cut along the outline. Bend the scored areas until the creases appear (12a). Score in between the raised creases. Fold the scored lines as if folding a fan, then flatten the piece out again (12b). Draw and cut out some smaller cloud shapes (12c). To finish, mount the pieces on or around the graffiti with tape loops (12d).

# Fish pond

Translucent vellum (which is known by several alternative names; see page 12) creates great depth of field, giving anything placed behind it a mysterious and dreamlike quality. This makes it one of my favourite papers to use. This project is an ideal introduction to vellum, and will also teach you about layering techniques and framing.

# You will need:

## Materials

- 2 photocopies of the master template on page 179, enlarged to 250%
- 1 photocopy of each template on pages 180-181, enlarged to 250%
- Assembly guides on pages 182-183, for reference
- Watercolour, gouache or acrylic paints in bright fish colours and black
- Wooden picture frame, 16 x 20in (40 x 50cm) with rabbet depth of at least 1½in (3.8cm)
- Dark-coloured mat board, 16 x 20in (40 x 50cm), for backboard
- Foam board, 20 x 30 x ³⁄₁₆ in (50cm x 76 x 0.5cm), for supports and spacers
- Masking tape, 1in (2.5cm) wide
- Glue
- Medium-weight dark green paper, 19 x 25in (48 x 63cm), for plants
- 55lb (90gsm) vellum paper, 16 x 20in (40 x 50cm), for water
- Green opaque decorative paper, 22 x 30in (56 x 76cm), for lily pads
- Medium-weight white paper, 19 x 25in (48 x 63cm), for fish and water lily
- Double-sided tape
- 8 or more offset clips (see page 40)
- Picture-framing wire
- 2 picture-frame hangers
- Screws

**Tip:** If you can work out how to separate the layers yourself (see page 26), you can save half the cost of making photocopies.

## Tools

- Cutting mat
- Jar of water
- Palettes or dishes
- Brush
- Metal ruler
- Craft knife
- Scissors (optional)
- Wire cutters
- Blanket
- Screwdriver

# Instructions:

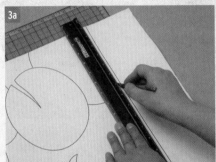

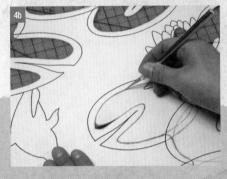

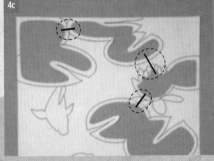

**Tip:** An oversize photocopy could be slightly out, so make sure you measure the photocopy and trim it accordingly.

1 Take the paints and the sheet of white paper. Cut the paper in half. Save one half for the flower and cut the other half in two. Paint both pieces of paper with random brushstrokes (1a). When you add black paint, wait until the first coat has dried, then apply the black paint over the colours (1b). Let the paint dry completely.

2 Prepare your picture frame with ¾in (19mm)-wide frame spacers (see page 38) (2). Then prepare a backboard with the mat board and 1in (2.5cm)-wide strips from the foam board (see page 39). Put them both to one side.

3 Take one of the master templates and trim it so that it is ¼in (6mm) smaller all around from the outline (3a), so that it can fit within the mat spacers. (See Tip, above right.) On the template, draw estimated lines to complete the shapes of all the hidden parts of the lily pads (3b).

4 Draw shapes within the outlines of each object that will sit above the vellum (that will be everything except for the fish), leaving at least a ¼in (6mm) border inside between the shape and the outline of the object. Connect the adjacent shapes (4a). Cut out the holes (4b). Make cuts on the template where indicated (4c).

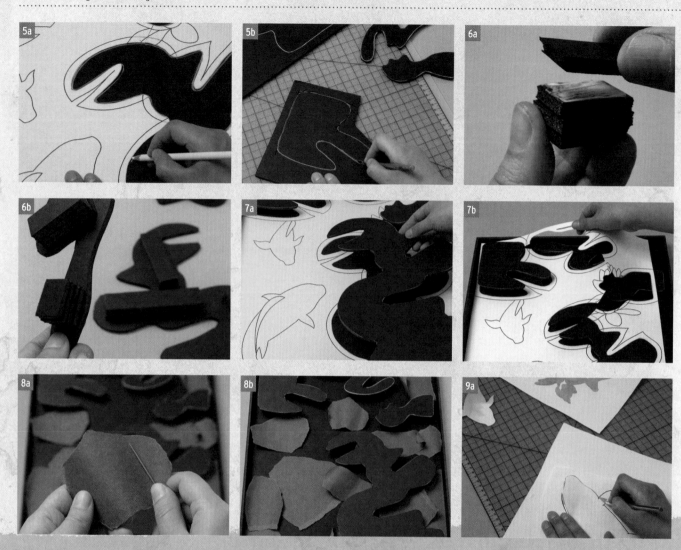

5 With masking tape, secure the cut master template onto a sheet of foam board. Draw inside the edges of the holes onto the foam board (5a). Put the template aside and cut the shapes out of the foam board (5b). You do not need to cut neatly; if cutting a curvy line is hard, make multiple straight cuts along the curved lines instead.

6 Cut small pieces of foam board and glue four of them together to create a little stack (6a). Evenly distribute one or more stacks onto the back of each foam shape to make foam supports that are about 1in (2.5cm) high (6b). It is important that the heights of the mat spacers and the foam supports are the same.

7 Take the backboard, and place it on your work surface taped side down. Centre the cut master template on the backboard. Put some glue on the back of the foam supports. Carefully position the supports, matching the holes on the template (7a). Hold them down until the glue sets. Carefully remove the template without tearing it (7b).

8 Take the sheet of dark green paper. Tear it into pieces of varying shapes and cut some strips too. Curl the shapes to different heights (see page 32) (8a). Glue them down on the board. This will create an illusion that there are lots of plants under water. Keep the pieces no higher than the mat spacers and foam board supports (8b).

9 Take the fish templates and the painted paper. Place the fish body templates onto the painted paper and secure them with masking tape. Cut the shapes out (9a). Curl away the edges of the fish bodies, except for the little fins and the tail (9b). Note that the fins are cut into the bodies a little so that the body edges can be curled while the fins stay flat.

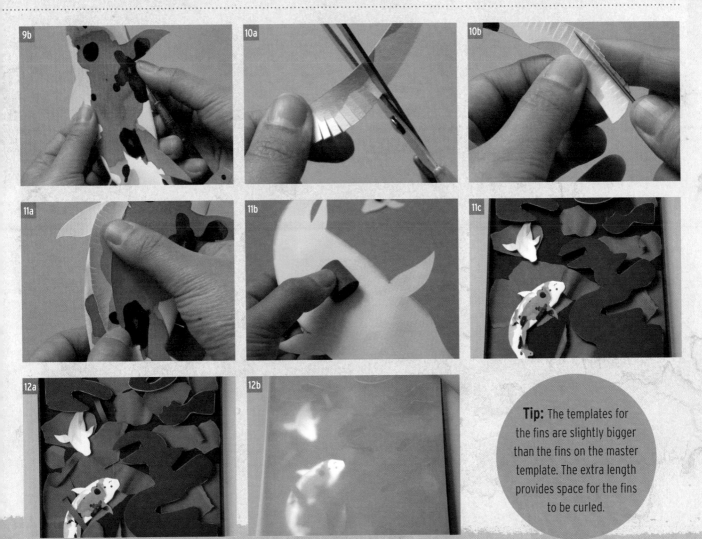

**Tip:** The templates for the fins are slightly bigger than the fins on the master template. The extra length provides space for the fins to be curled.

10 Now cut the fins out, using the fin templates. Make partial cuts about ⅛in (3mm) apart along the fins, leaving a little space on the bottom for gluing. These cuts are helpful when you curl the curved fin for the big fish (10a); they also make them look more 'fin-like' under the vellum. (See Tip above right.) Curl the fins upwards (10b).

11 Put a dab of glue on the bottom edge of the fins and attach them along the spines of the fish (11a). Make two looped supports (see page 34) out of green paper and glue one to the back of each fish to give them some height (11b). Now glue the fish to the board, using the master template as a reference for the position (11c).

12 Place some more torn paper and strips over and around the fish and finish covering the board. Keep everything below the supports level (12a). Handling it with care, lay a sheet of vellum on top of the mat spacers to see if anything sticks up too much (12b). Put the vellum to one side.

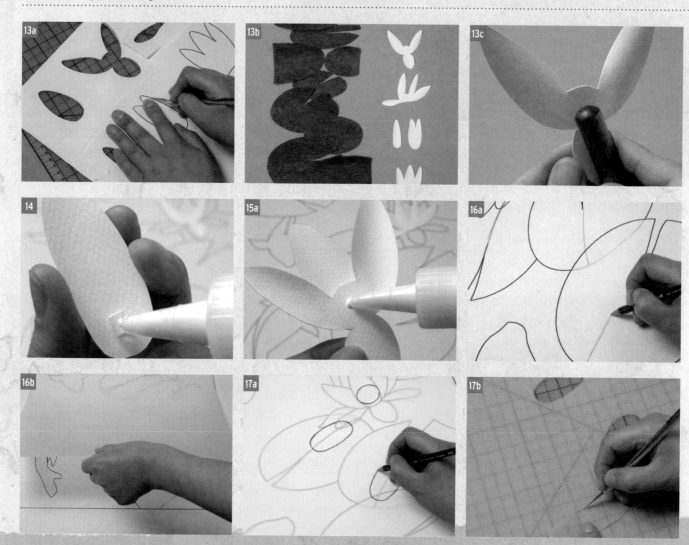

13 Take the templates for the water-lily petals and pads, the white paper, and the green decorative paper. Using masking tape, secure each template onto the corresponding paper. Cut out the shapes (13a) (13b). Create a little curl on the petals lengthwise. Referring to the illustration on page 182 for guidance, curl the foreground petals away from you and the background petals and fully opened petals towards you (13c).

14 Place the uncut master template onto your work surface. To assemble the flower, place petal 2 on the master template, matching the guidelines as shown on the illustration on page 182. On the back of petal 1, attach a small white looped support (14). Glue it to petal 2. Put it to one side.

15 Position petal 3 on the template. Put glue on the back of the previously assembled petals and attach them to petal 3 without a support (15a). Assemble the rest of the flower as shown in the diagram on page 182, without a support.

16 On the master template, draw middle ribs on each lily pad (16a). Take the vellum and position it on the template (16b). Secure the vellum to the master template with low-tack masking tape (see page 26). Test it on a scrap of vellum to make sure that the tape won't tear the vellum.

17 Within the outlines of the lily pads, draw 1in (2.5cm)-wide oblong shapes centred along the middle ribs on the vellum. Draw a circle within the flower (17a). Remove the master template and tapes. Cut all the holes out of the vellum (17b).

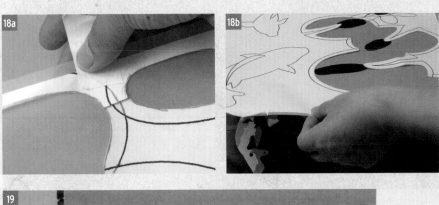

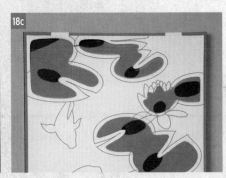

**Tip:** A clean-cut wedge of foam board or mat board works well for spreading out glue.

18 Put the vellum on a clean work surface. Take the cut master template. Carefully hold the cut master template and centre it on the vellum. Secure it with some low-tack masking tape (18a). On the mat spacers, position the vellum and template (18b) and secure them. Make sure the edges of the vellum sit evenly on all of the spacers (18c).

19 Thinly apply glue to the exposed supports (19). Be careful not to glue the vellum, as it is very sensitive to moisture and the moisture in your glue can wrinkle the paper. Note that even if you use a dry adhesive, such as double-sided tape, the combination of changes in humidity and a difference in tension between the adhered area and free area will cause the paper to warp.

**20** Attach the lily pads to the support, matching the guideline (20a). After attaching the first batch of lily pads, glue the second batch (20b), then the last lily pad and the flower (20c). Glue any lily pads that are hanging out too much to the overlapping pad (20d).

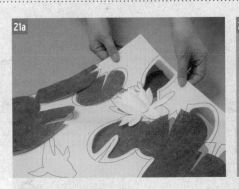

21 After the glue has dried completely, carefully remove the tape and the template (21a). Trim any paper that is sticking out of the mat spacers (21b). Put a blanket on your work surface and place the artwork on it. Hold the frame front side up and put it over the sculpture (21c). Keep the vellum positioned evenly on the spacers. Matching corner to corner, carefully press it down. Hold the frame and your artwork altogether and turn them over. Finish framing as directed on page 42 (21d).

# Hummingbird

Hummingbirds have long been one of my favourite subjects for
paper sculptures. This project will be challenging because the
materials are so delicate and worked on a small scale. Every cut
and every layer adds to the texture, which translates into
the jewel-like quality of the hummingbird. Try skipping
some of the finer details on your first attempt so you
can build up your skills gradually.

# You will need:

## Materials

- 1 photocopy of each template on pages 184-185, reproduced at 100%
- 1 sheet of medium-weight white cardstock for the body base and the eye
- Masking tape
- 1 sheet of white mat board, 8½ x 11in (21.6 x 28cm) and about 1/16in (1.5mm) thick, for the armatures
- 1 sheet of white tissue paper, at least 8½ x 11in (21.6 x 28cm), for the wings
- 1 sheet of clear overlay film, big enough to cover the master template
- Glue
- 1 sheet of white Japanese paper, at least 8½ x 11in (21.6 x 28cm), for the feathers
- Removable adhesive, sticky disc type (see page 15)

## Tools

- Craft knife
- Cutting mat
- Awl
- Tweezers
- French curve

# Instructions:

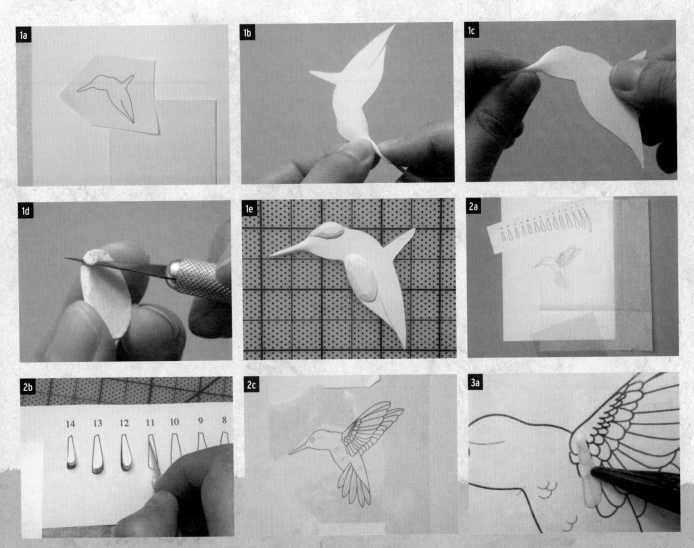

1 Take the body base template, the white cardstock, and a piece of mat board (1a). Secure the template on the cardstock with masking tape and cut along the outline of the body base. Curl the beak away lengthwise with an awl (1b). Then gently squeeze the beak with your fingers to shape it (1c). Cut the armatures out of mat board. Carve the edges of the pieces to make smooth convex surfaces (1d). Glue the armatures to the base (1e).

2 Take the master template, the feather A templates, the tissue paper and a sheet of clear overlay film (2a). Secure the feather A templates with masking tape to a sheet of tissue paper and cut along the outlines except for the feather bases (2b). Place the master template on your work surface and secure the clear overlay film over the template with masking tape (2c).

3 Cut the bases of feathers A14 and 13. Secure feather A14 by gluing the base to the film with a dab of glue, matching the guideline on the master template (3a). Apply glue along the edge of A14 where it overlaps with A13. Keep the glue within the feather B and C. Attach A13 to A14, matching the guideline on the template; position with tweezers if necessary.

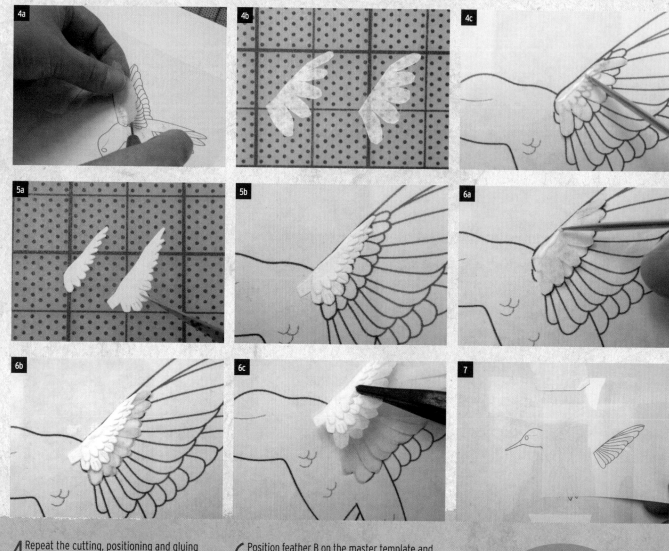

4 Repeat the cutting, positioning and gluing process on the rest of feather A. Let the glue dry completely. Slide an awl under the feathers and gently lift the assembled feathers from the film (4a). Put the feathers aside. Cut feather B1 and B2 out of tissue paper (4b). Position B2 on the master template (4c). Glue B1 to B2 on the straight edge.

5 Take the template for feathers C1 and C2 and the Japanese paper and cut out the feathers. Make one or two short cuts on the bigger scallops (5a). Position feather C2 on the template, and apply glue along the straight edge. Attach feather C1 to the C2, forming offset patterns (5b).

6 Position feather B on the master template and apply glue on the straight edge (6a). Attach feather C to feather B, matching the guideline (6b). Put them aside. Position feather A on the film and put glue on the base of the feathers. Attach feathers B and C to feather A (6c). Put the wing to one side.

7 Take the background wing and wing feathers template and the tissue paper. Cut around the wing template, and slide it under the film over the master template (7). Repeat the cutting and gluing process from step 3, starting with the background feather templates 1 and 2. Put the wing aside. Remove the wing template.

**Tip:** Cut a piece of the overlay film to use for a glue reservoir. When the glue dries up, just peel it off, and you can then reuse the film.

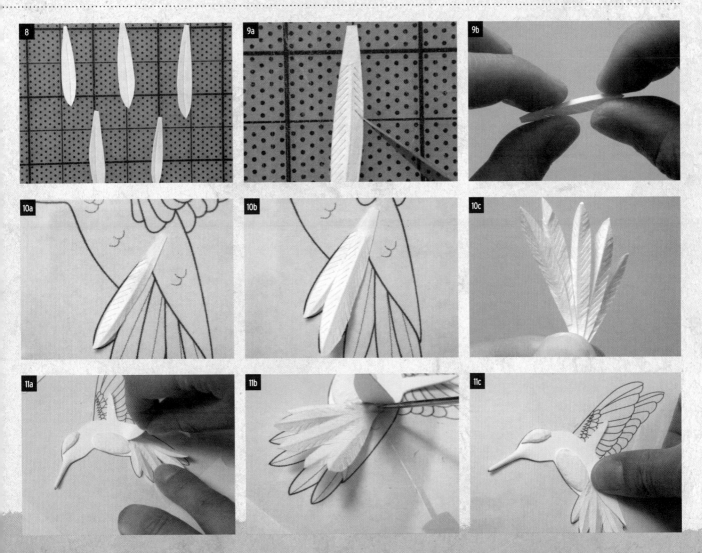

8 Take the tail-feather templates and secure them on the Japanese paper. Firmly score the crease lines, using a French curve. Cut out all of the feathers (8). Turn them over and bend the scored areas away from you, so that raised creases appear. Note that the tail-feather templates are reversed. If your paper has different textures on each side, secure the templates accordingly.

9 On each feather, make diagonal short cuts downwards along one side of the crease, starting from where the crease starts (9a). Repeat on the other side. Reshape the feathers by bending the creases (9b). If the tail feather gets bent and loses the stiffness, reinforce it by applying glue on the back where it is bent. Let the glue dry.

10 Position the base of feather 5 on the master template and glue the feather base to the film (10a). On the back of feather 4, apply glue to the base. Position and glue feather 4 to feather 5 (10b). Repeat the same process to assemble the rest of the tail feathers. Carefully take the tail off the film (10c).

11 Take the body base, and secure it on the film with a little glue. Open up the slot on the body base and slide the tail under (11a). Apply glue to the tail base (11b) then close up the slot, applying some pressure on the glued area (11c).

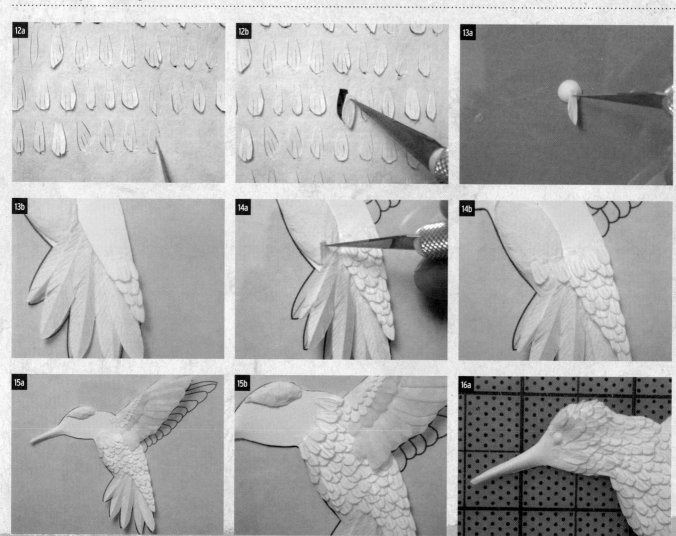

12 To make the body feathers, take the Japanese paper and make cuts about ¼in (6mm) long and in various widths - as many as you can fit on the paper - leaving the feather bases uncut (12a). Squeeze out a drop of glue onto a clean surface. Cut out one of the body feathers (12b).

13 Pick up the body feather with the blade of a knife. Gently dip the back of the feather base into the glue, so that only a tiny bit of glue gets on the feather base (13a). Start gluing the feather to the body base from the rear end, covering the edges. Keep cutting and gluing the body feathers one next to another in scallop patterns (13b).

14 When you have covered the body base up to the point where tail feather 5 is, start covering the abdomen side of the body, too, just under tail feather 5 (14a). Keep cutting the body feathers as required; you don't need to cover places that will not be visible when everything is assembled (14b).

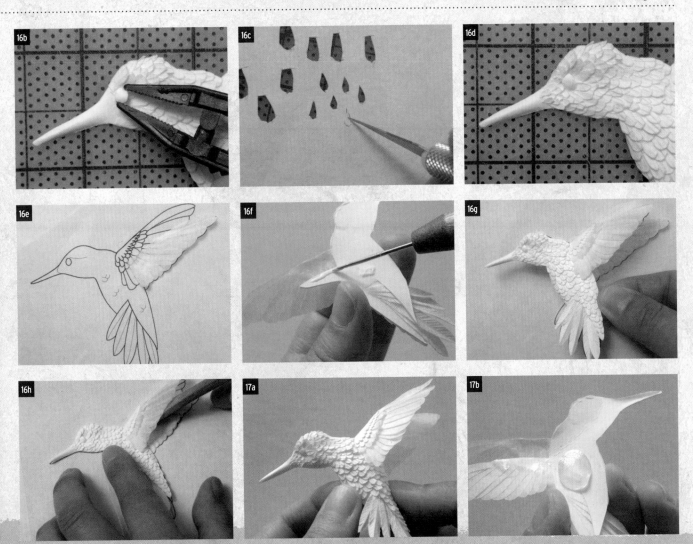

15 When you reach where the foreground wing is, take the foreground wing and glue the base of the wing to the body base (15a). Keep covering the body including the base of the wing (15b). Detach the bird, and keep covering the head until you reach the spot for the eye. Cut the eye out of cardstock and emboss it on the back with a stylus.

16 Apply a drop of glue about the size of the eye on the body base (16a). Carefully place the eye on the glue, and let go (16b). Cut out tiny teardrop shapes (16c), and cover the rest of the head up to the base of the beak (16d). Position the background wing on the master template, and secure the base to the film with glue (16e). Put glue on the back of the wing base (16f). Position the wing base to the background wing (16g). Burnish the glued area (16h).

17 Detach the bird. Bend the edges of the back and neck to create curves for a more natural look (17a). Attach a piece of removable adhesive to the back of the bird (17b) and affix it where you want it displayed. Note that it is best to avoid draughty or high-traffic places. Lastly, fluff up the body feathers by lifting them with an awl.

# Templates

NOTE: MASTER TEMPLATES AND ASSEMBLY DIAGRAMS ARE IN BLACK.  CUTTING, EMBOSSING AND SCORING LINES ARE IN GREY.

## Project 1: Butterfly

INSTRUCTIONS: PHOTOCOPY AT A SIZE TO FIT IN YOUR FRAME

Template 1

Template 2

# Project 2: Snake

**INSTRUCTIONS: PHOTOCOPY AT A SIZE TO FIT IN YOUR FRAME**

Master template

Head

Body

Tail

# Project 3: Pop-up card
**INSTRUCTIONS: PHOTOCOPY BOTH TEMPLATES AT 150%**

## Template 1: Fence

# Template 2: Clothesline

## Assembly 1

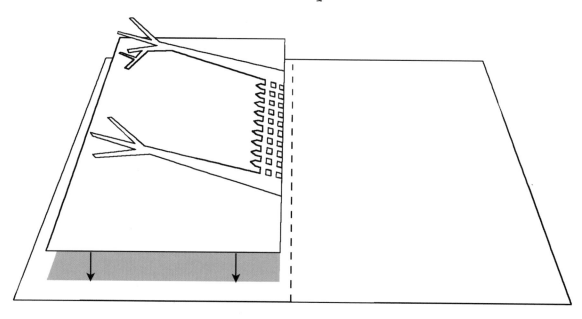

## Assembly 2

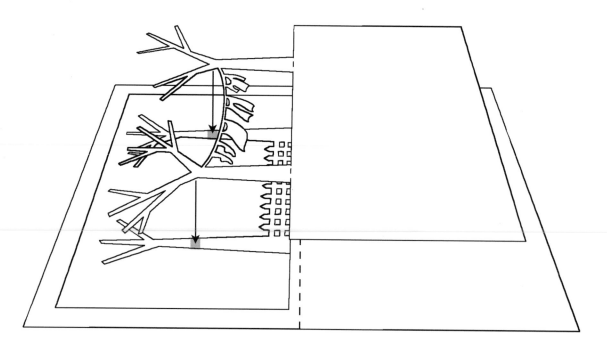

## Assembly 3

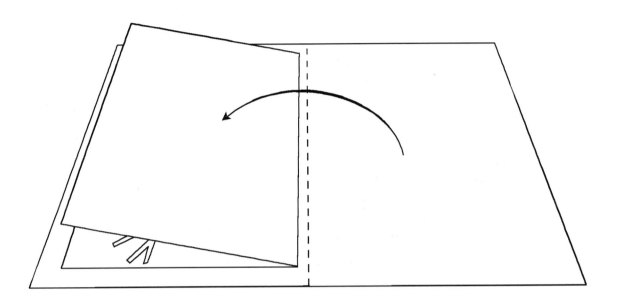

## Assembly 4

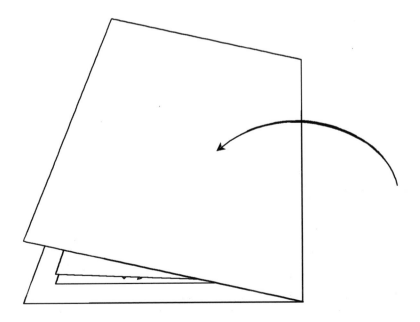

## Assembly 5

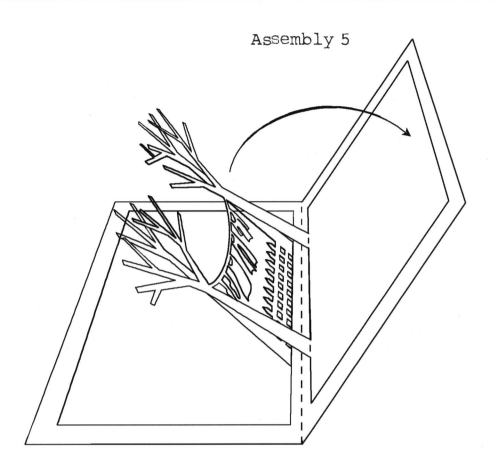

## Assembly 6

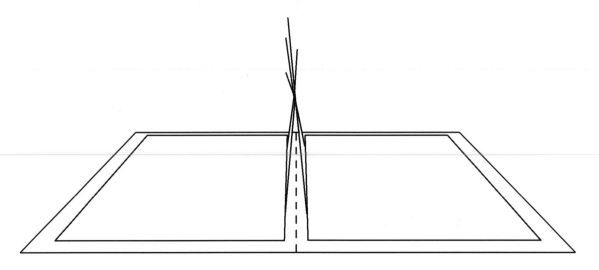

# Project 4: Music plaque

**INSTRUCTIONS: THIS IS FOR REFERENCE ONLY**

Treble clefs

Time signature

Semibreve

Minims

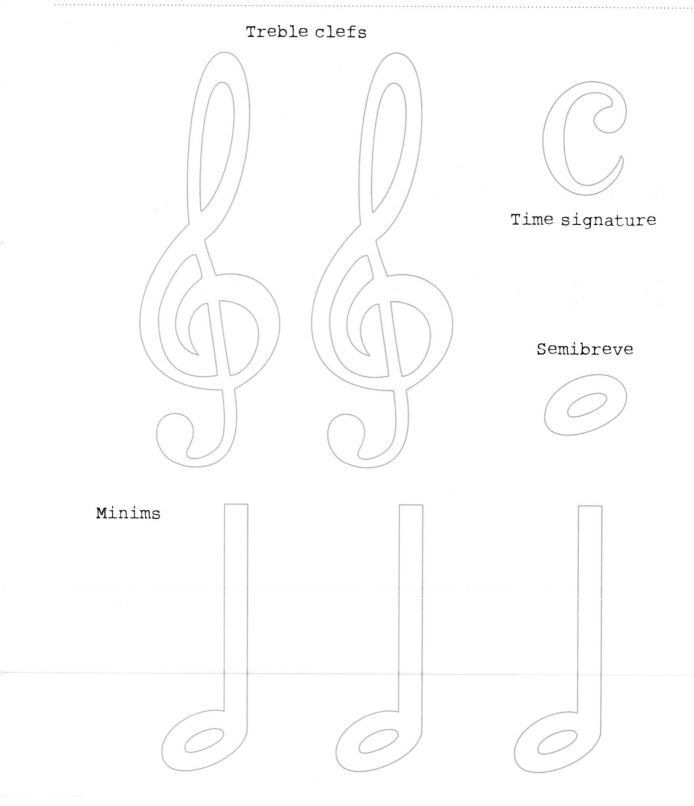

# Crochets

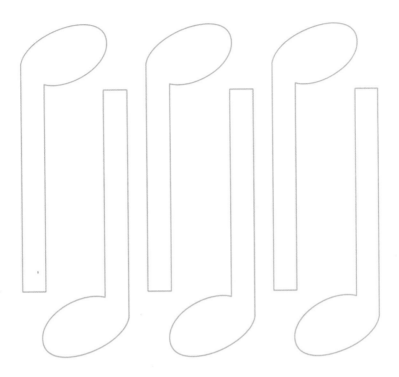

# Bar lines

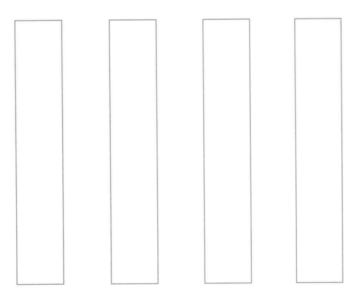

## Lamb 1

Fleece

Hair

Base

Head

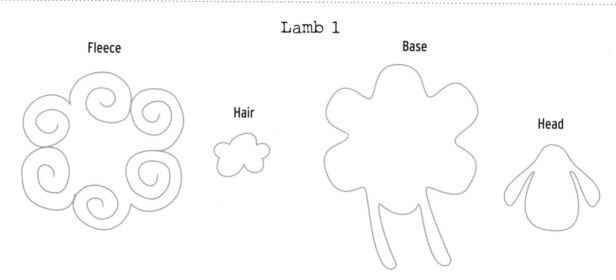

## Lamb 2

Fleece

Ear slot

Base

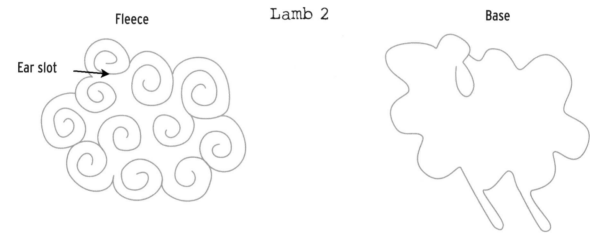

## Lamb 3

Fleece

Ear slot

Base

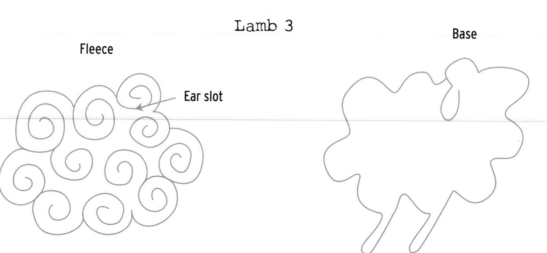

# Project 5: Kraken & submarine
**INSTRUCTIONS: PHOTOCOPY AT A SIZE TO FIT IN YOUR CLOCK FRAME**

Background template

**Seaweed**

**Reef**

**Jellyfish 1**

**Jellyfish 2**

**Jellyfish 3**

**Fish**

**Starfish**

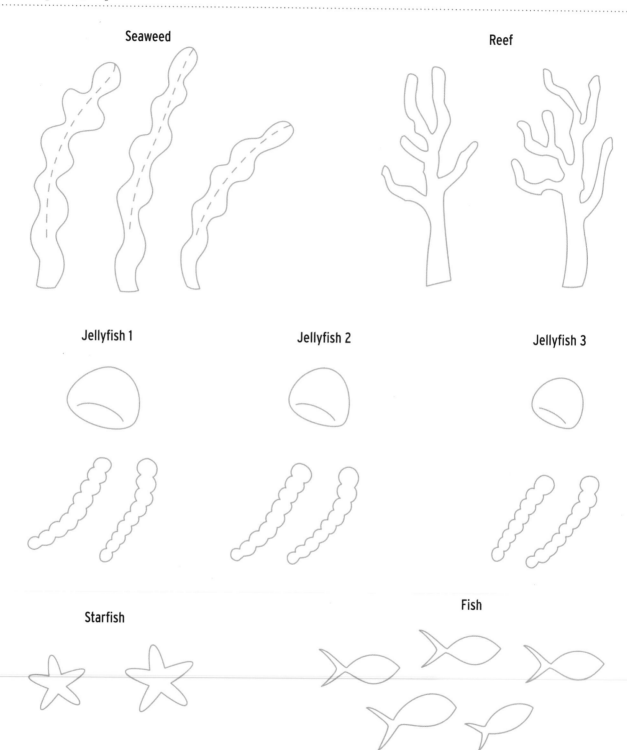

# Kraken

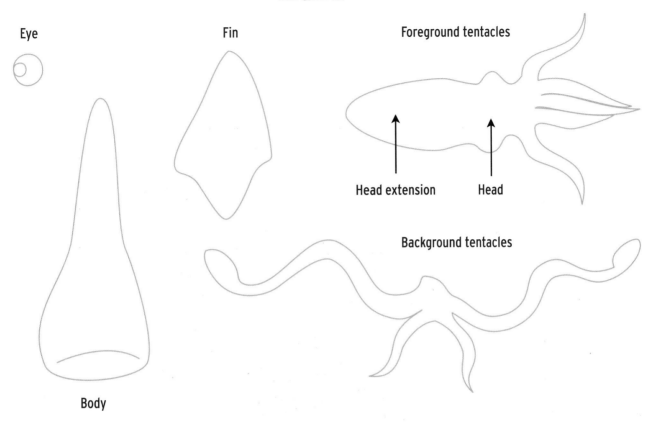

**Eye**

**Fin**

**Foreground tentacles**

Head extension    Head

**Body**

**Background tentacles**

# Submarine

**Submarine body**

**Periscope**

**Propeller**

**Window**

# Project 6: The owl & the pussycat
**INSTRUCTIONS: PHOTOCOPY AT 100%**

Master template

# Background

# Waves

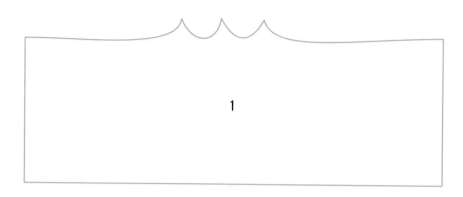

1

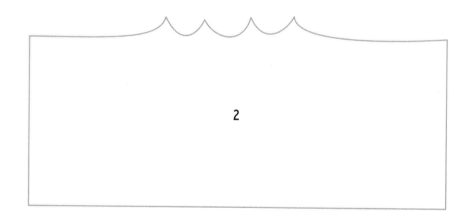

2

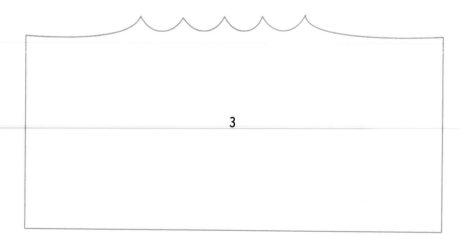

3

# Heart

# Boat

# Guitar

A

B

# Project 7: Coat of arms
## INSTRUCTIONS: ENLARGE TO 300%

Master template

# Shield

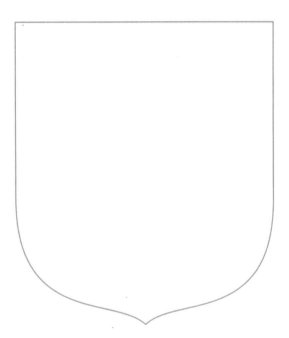

# Banner

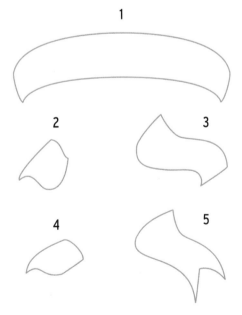

# Symbols

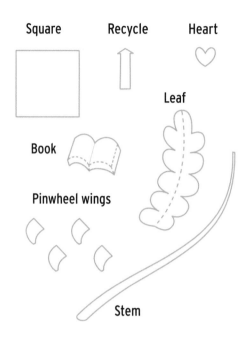

Square    Recycle    Heart

Leaf

Book

Pinwheel wings

Stem

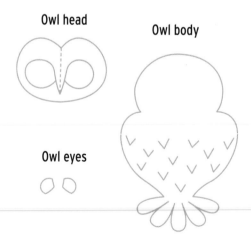

Owl head    Owl body

Owl eyes

Mouse body    Foreground    Background
                    ear            ear

# Sample letters

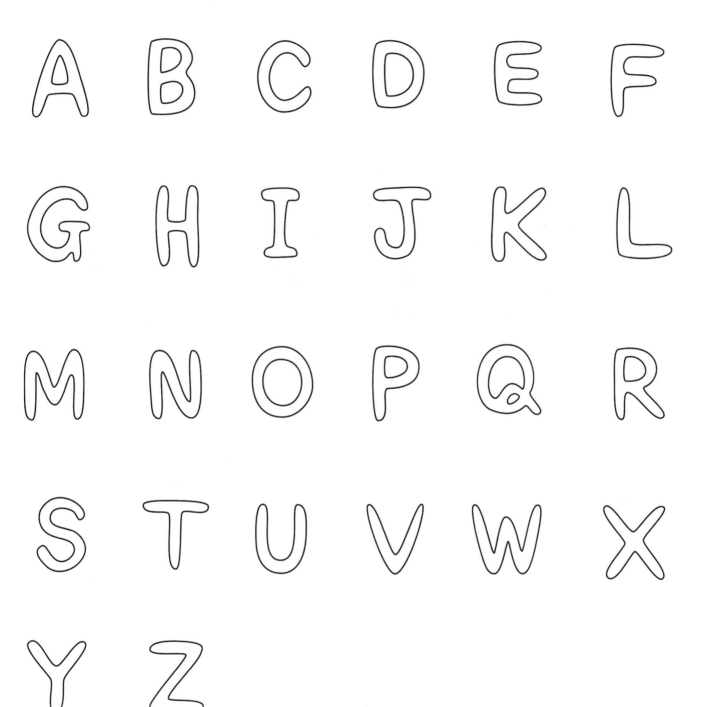

# Project 8: Architectural ornament
## INSTRUCTIONS: ENLARGE TO 450%

Master template

Waves

# Shell

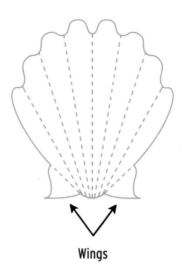

**Wings**

# Fish

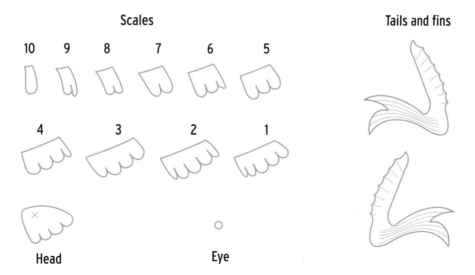

**Scales**

10   9   8   7   6   5

4   3   2   1

**Head**          **Eye**

**Tails and fins**

# Project 9: Trumpet flowers

## INSTRUCTIONS: 3 TEMPLATES TO BE REPRODUCED AT 100%

Master template

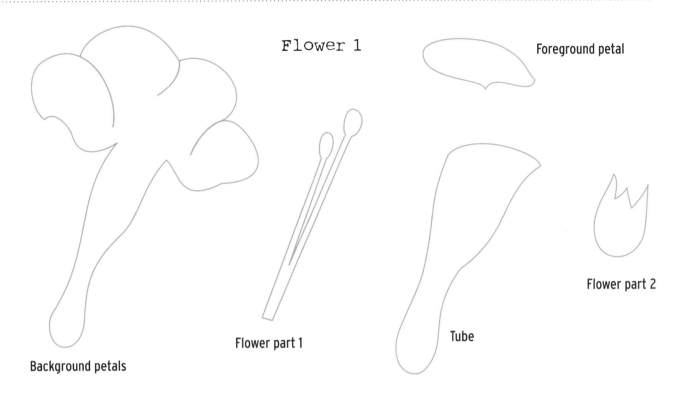

Flower 1

Foreground petal

Flower part 2

Flower part 1

Tube

Background petals

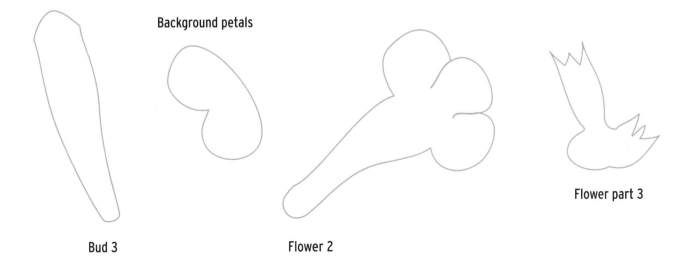

Flower 2 and Bud 3

Background petals

Flower part 3

Bud 3

Flower 2

# Bud 1 and Bud 2

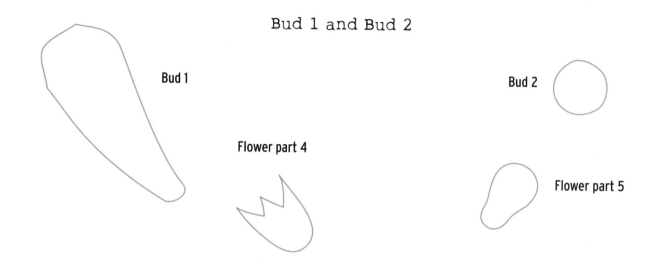

Bud 1

Bud 2

Flower part 4

Flower part 5

# Leaf 2

# Leaf 3

# Leaf 1

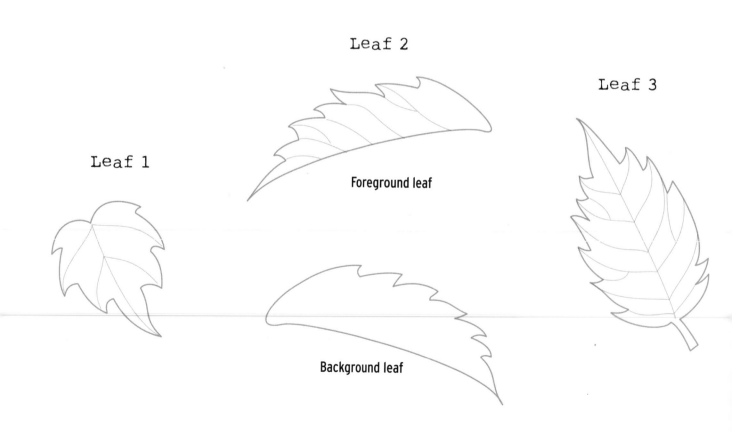

Foreground leaf

Background leaf

# Embossing map Flower 1

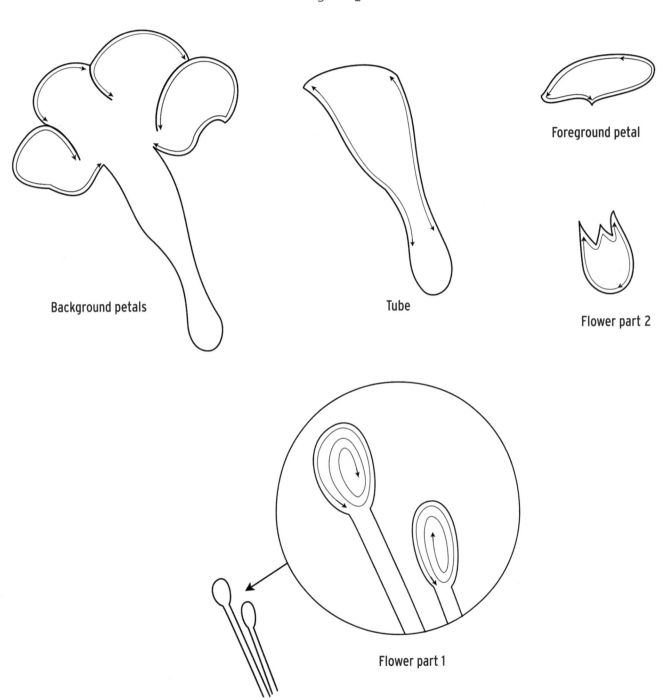

Background petals

Tube

Foreground petal

Flower part 2

Flower part 1

# Flower 2 and Bud 3

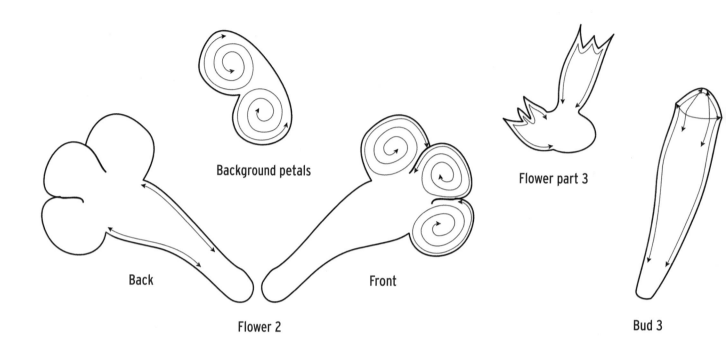

Background petals

Flower part 3

Back

Front

Flower 2

Bud 3

# Bud 1 and Bud 2

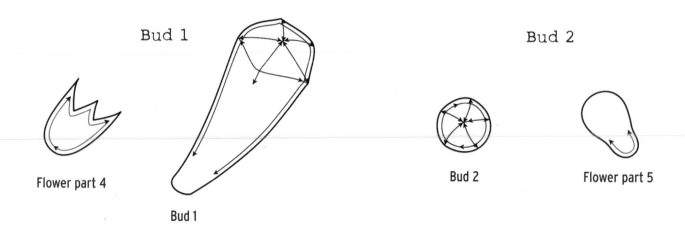

Bud 1

Bud 2

Flower part 4

Bud 1

Bud 2

Flower part 5

# Project 10: Beetle specimen
## INSTRUCTIONS: SIZED TO FIT IN YOUR CONTAINER

Master template

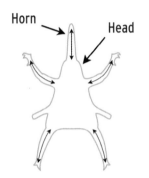

Head and legs

Thorax

Outer wings

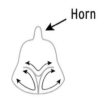

Upper abdomen

Inner wings

Lower abdomen

# Project 11: Cameo
## INSTRUCTIONS: USE THIS TEMPLATE OR CREATE YOUR OWN

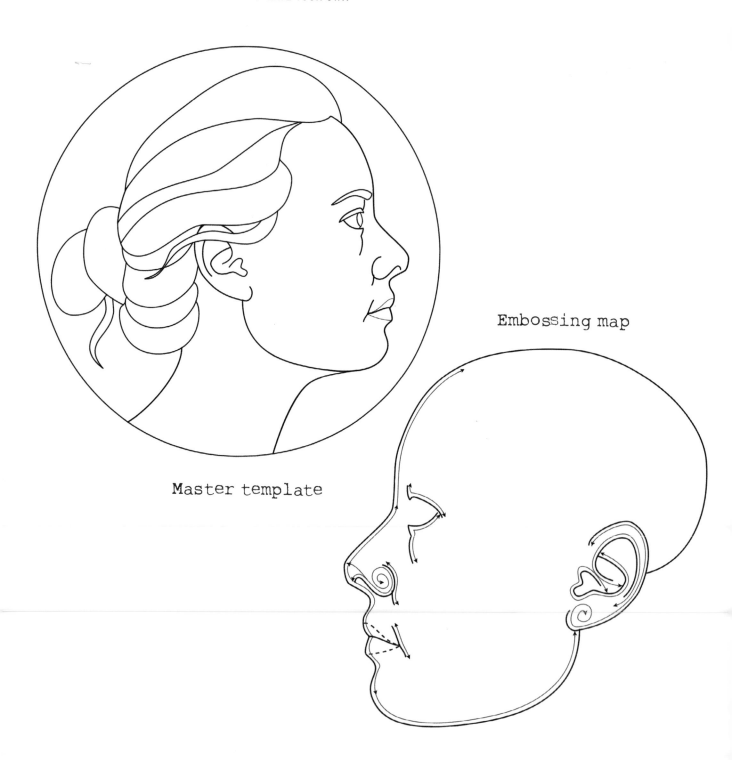

Master template

Embossing map

# Project 12: Dog portrait

**INSTRUCTIONS: USE THIS TEMPLATE OR CREATE YOUR OWN**

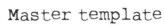

Master template

# Embossing map

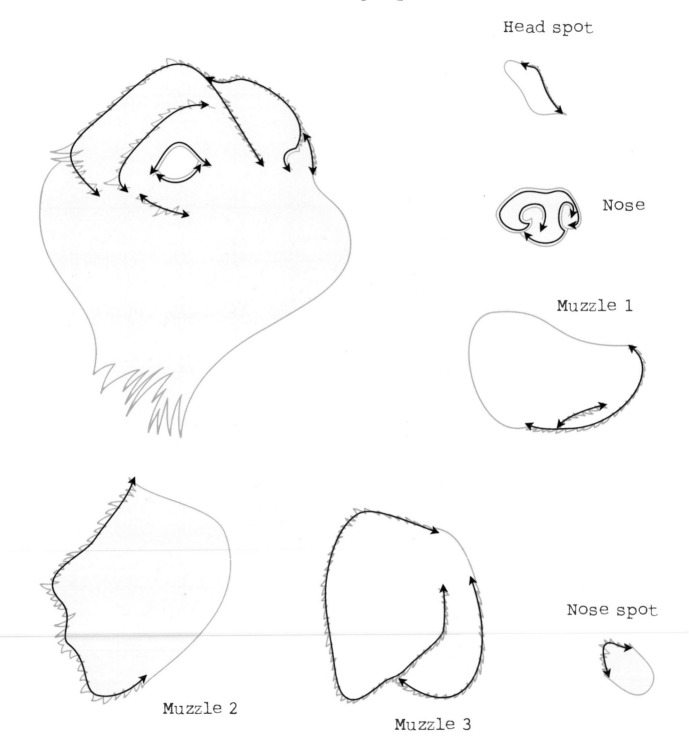

Head spot

Nose

Muzzle 1

Muzzle 2

Muzzle 3

Nose spot

# Guidance for layers

## Neck

## Head

## Head spot

# Muzzle

## Nose

## Nose spot

## Ears

# Eyes

# Project 13: Graffiti

**INSTRUCTIONS: USE THIS TEMPLATE OR CREATE YOUR OWN**

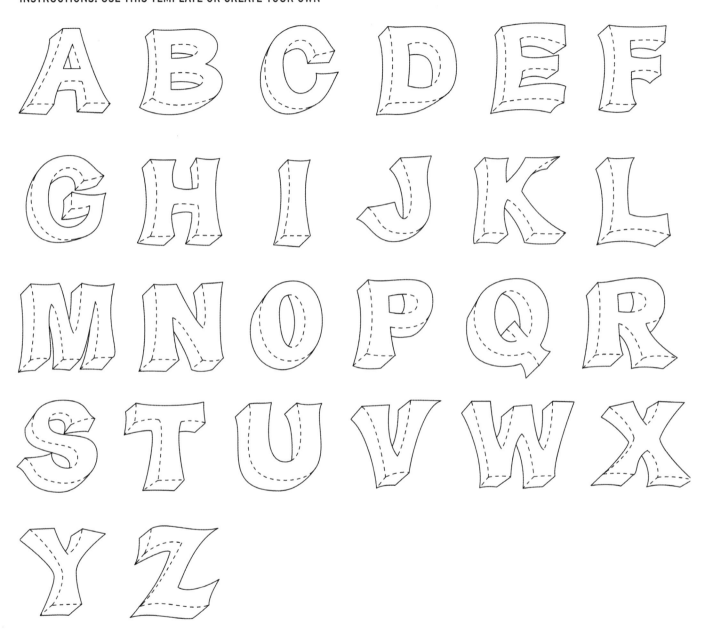

# Starburst

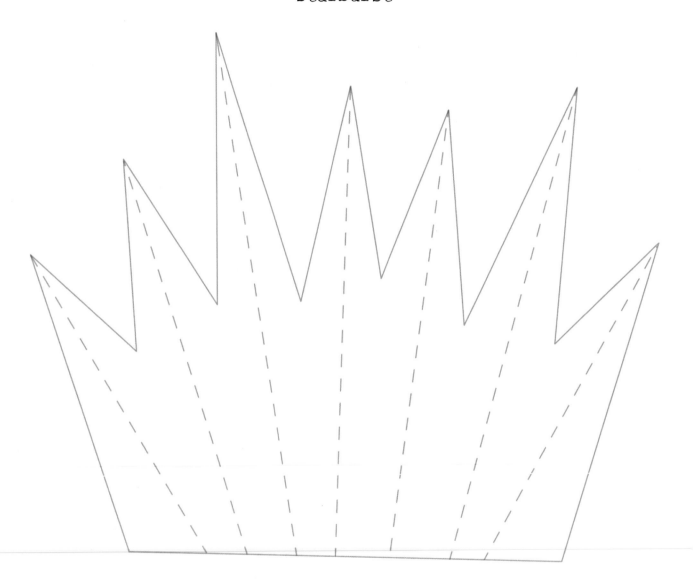

# Project 14: Fish pond

## Master template

**INSTRUCTIONS: ENLARGE TO 250%**

# Lily pad

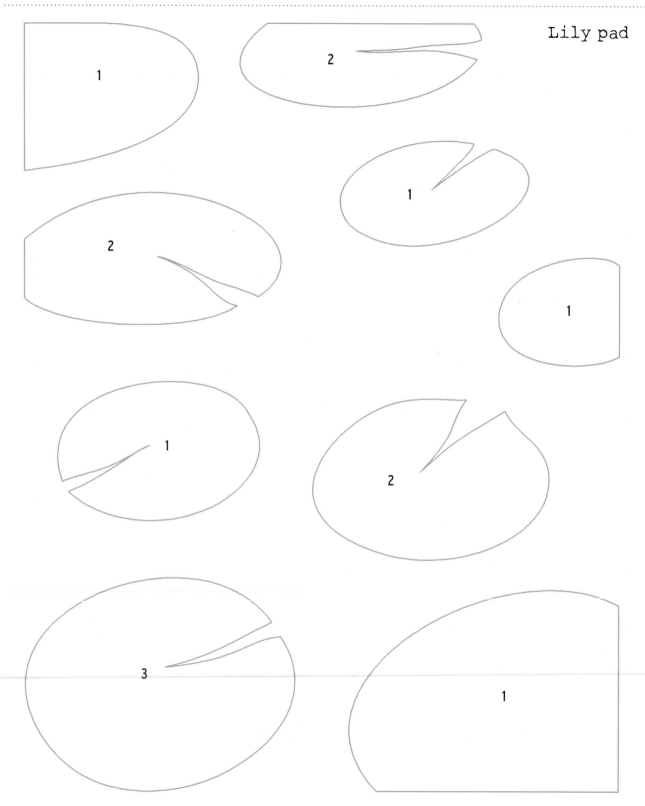

# Fish

# Petals

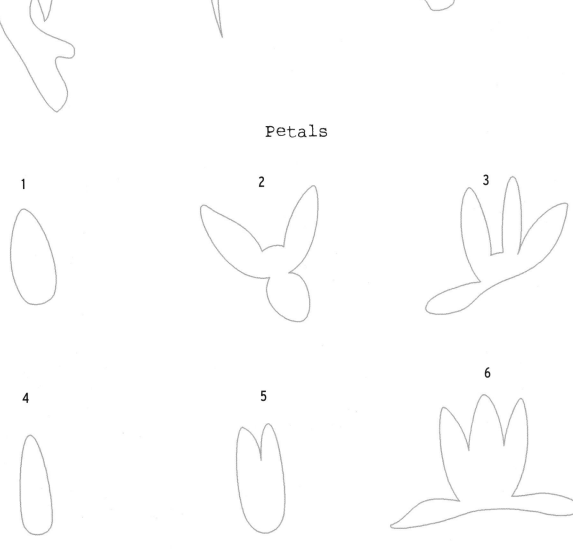

# Assembly guides

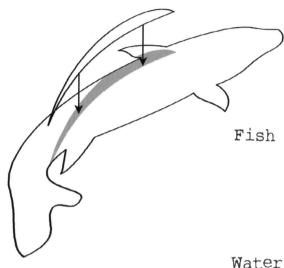

### Fish

## Water lily

**Background petals**

**Foreground petals**

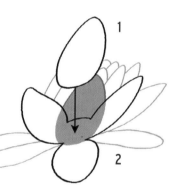

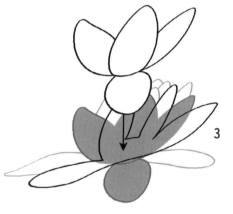

**Fully opened petals**

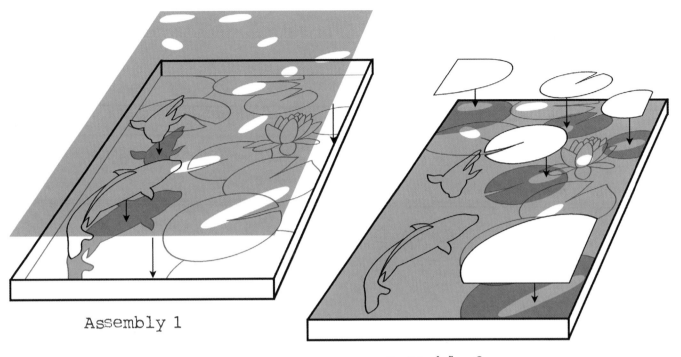

Assembly 1

Assembly 2

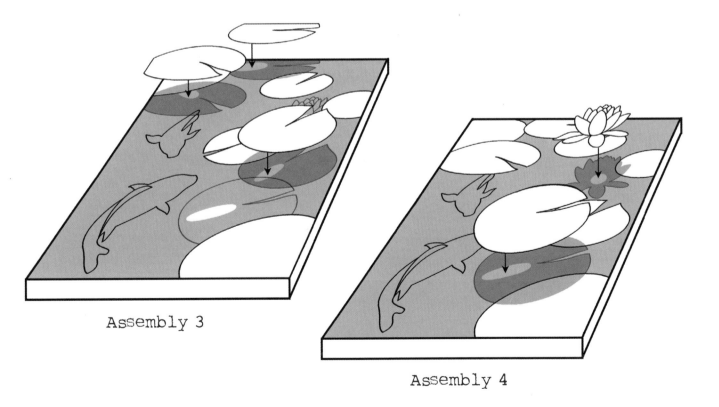

Assembly 3

Assembly 4

# Project 15: Hummingbird
INSTRUCTIONS: REPRODUCE AT 100%

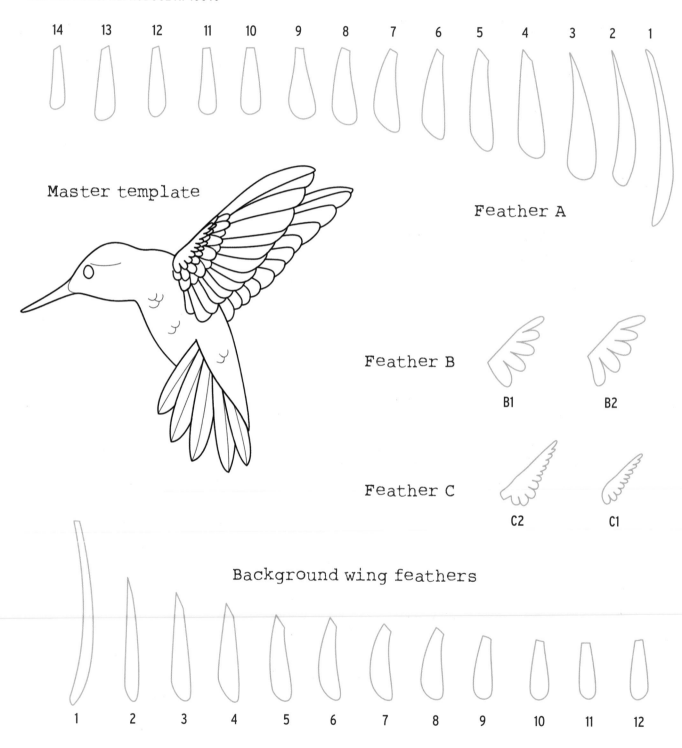

14  13  12  11  10  9  8  7  6  5  4  3  2  1

Feather A

Master template

Feather B

B1          B2

Feather C

C2          C1

Background wing feathers

1   2   3   4   5   6   7   8   9   10   11   12

# Armatures

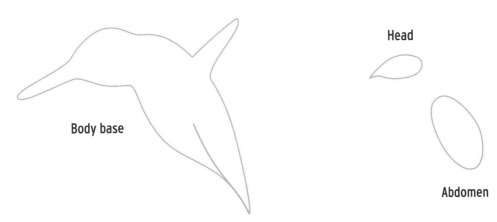

**Body base**

**Head**

**Abdomen**

# Tail feathers

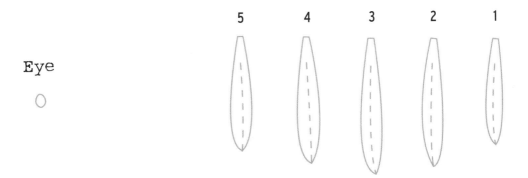

**Eye**

# Background wing

# Suppliers

## Australia

**A1 Framing Supplies Warehouse**
8/104 Newmarket Road
Windsor
Queensland 4030
www.a1frames.com.au
Tel: +61 (0)7 3357 3022

**Art Material Supplies**
Wide Bay Gallery
PO Box 1218
Maryborough
Queensland 4650
www.artmaterialsupplies.com
Tel: +61 (0)7 4122 1858
International orders: worldwide

**Art Materials**
PO Box 3261
Mornington
Victoria 3931
Tel: +61 1300 552 390

**Art Shed Brisbane**
274 Montague Road (corner of Scott Street)
West End
Queensland 4101
www.artshedbrisbane.com.au
Tel: +61 (0)7 3846 1330

**The Art Shop**
Unit 4, 21 Power Road
Bayswater
Victoria 3153
www.theartshop.com.au
Tel: +61 (3) 9758 3266; 1800 444 419
International orders: worldwide

**Australian Art Supplies**
1935B Pittwater Road
Bayview
New South Wales 2104
www.australianartsupplies.com.au
Tel: +61 (0)2 9999 0669

**Newtown Art Supplies**
15 Wilson Street
Newtown
Sydney
New South Wales 2042
www.newtownartsupplies.com.au
Tel: +61 (0)2 9516 2339

**The Online Picture Framing Shop**
85-89 Chapel Street
Roselands
New South Wales 2196
www.frameshop.com.au
Tel: +61 (0)2 9750 6055

**Riot Art & Craft**
See website for store addresses
www.riotstores.com.au

## Thailand
**Intirado**
www.etsy.com/shop/Intirado
International orders: worldwide

## UK
**3D Decoupage & Frames**
Tanyfoel
Cwmsymlog
Aberystwyth SY23 3HA
www.decoupage-frames.co.uk
Tel: +44 (0)1970 820308
International orders: worldwide

**Art Discount**
www.artdiscount.co.uk
Tel: 0800 999 2100; +44 (0)1253 624402
International orders: worldwide

**Artists Materials Online**
The Art Centre
Florence Road Business Park
Kelly Bray
Callington
Cornwall PL17 8EX
www.artistsmaterialsonline.co.uk
Tel: +44 (0)1579 383523
International orders: mainland Europe & EFTA countries

**Atlantis Art Materials & Art Supplies**
Britannia House
68-80 Hanbury Street
London E1 5JL
www.atlantisart.co.uk
Tel: +44 (0)20 7377 8855
International orders: worldwide

**BoxFrames**
Unit 2c, Victoria Farm Estate
Water Lane
York YO30 6PQ
www.boxframes.co.uk
Tel: +44 (0)1904 693774

**eFrame**
20 Howard Road
Eaton Socon Industrial Estate
Cambs PE19 8ET
www.eframe.co.uk
Tel: +44 (0)1480 214777

**EzeFrame**
www.ezeframe.co.uk
Tel: +44 (0)1234 742166

**GreatArt**
*www.greatart.co.uk*
Tel: 8433 571 572; +44 (0)1420 59 3332

**Jackson's Art Supplies**
1 Farleigh Place
London N16 7SX
*www.jacksonsart.com*
Tel: +44 0844 499 8430
International orders: worldwide

**Ken Bromley Art Supplies**
Unit 13, Lodge Bank Estate
Crown Lane
Horwich
Bolton
Lancs BL6 5HY
*www.artsupplies.co.uk*
Tel: +44 (0)1204 690114
International orders: worldwide

**Moonshine Framing Penzance**
1 High Street
Penzance
Cornwall TR18 2SX
*www.frames.uk.com*
Tel: +44 (0)1736 330887

**PicFrames**
*www.picframes.co.uk*
Tel: +44 (0)1270 625 675

**Picture Frames Express**
304 Kingfield Road
Coventry CV1 4EP
*www.pictureframesexpress.co.uk*
Tel: +44 (0)2476 593529
International orders: worldwide

**Picture Hangers**
Unit F, Midland Road Ind Estate
Swadlincote
Derbyshire DE11 0AN
*www.picturehangers.co.uk*
Tel: +44 (0)1283 210 222

**USA**
**Antiqued**
*www.etsy.com/shop/Antiqued*
International orders: worldwide

**Archivers Annex**
*www.archiversannex.com*
Tel: 1 866 299 8229
International orders: Australia, UK, Canada

**CheapBoutique**
*www.etsy.com/shop/CheapBoutique*
International orders: worldwide

**Dick Blick Art Materials**
*www.dickblick.com*
Tel: 1 800 828 4548
International orders: worldwide
Tel: 1 309 343 6181

**FrameUSA**
225 Northland Blvd
Cincinnati
Ohio 45246
*www.frameusa.com*
Tel: 1 800 577 5920

**HHHdesigns**
*www.etsy.com/shop/HHHdesigns*
International orders: worldwide

**Hobby Lobby**
*www.hobbylobby.com*
Tel: 1 800 888 0321
International orders: 1 405 745 1275

**irismorgan**
*www.etsy.com/shop/irismorgan*
International orders: worldwide

**Jo-Ann Fabric and Craft Stores**
*www.joann.com*
Tel: 1 888 739 4120
International orders: USA & Canada

**Michaels Arts and Crafts**
*www.michaels.com*
Tel: 1 800 642 435
International orders: USA & Canada

**Papermart**
2164 N. Batavia Street
Orange
California 92865-3104
*www.papermart.com*
Tel: 1 800 745 8800

**pictureframes**
*www.pictureframes.com*
Tel: 1 800 332 8884
International orders: worldwide

**SKS Bottle & Packaging**
*www.sks-bottle.com*
Tel: 1 518 880 6980
International orders: worldwide

**Specialty Bottle**
3434 4th Avenue S
Seattle
Washington 98134
*www.specialtybottle.com*
Tel: 206 382 1100
International orders: worldwide

**Utrecht Art Supplies**
*www.utrechtart.com*
Tel: 1 800 223 9132
International orders: 1 609 409 8001

# Further reading

Kathleen Ziegler and Nick Greco,
**More Paper Sculpture: A Step-by Step Guide**
HarperCollins, 1997

Jane Thomas and Paul Jackson,
**On Paper: New Paper Art**
Merrell Publishers, 2001

Kathleen Ziegler and Nick Greco,
**Paper Sculpture: A Step-by-Step Guide**
HarperCollins, 1994

**The Paper Sculpture Book**
Independent Curators International,
New York, 2003

# Websites

*www.artisaway.com*
Includes paper designs of Elsa Mara (Elsita)

*www.jenstark.com*
Jen Stark's work, including paper cutting

*www.misterrob.co.uk*
Robert Ryan's site, including paper-cutting work

*www.paperforest.blogspot.com*
Work from a variety of paper-cutting artists

*www.sherchristopher.com*
The work of Sher Christopher, paper sculptor

# About the author

I live in Columbus, Ohio, in the USA with my husband and son. I was born in Seoul, South Korea, in 1970, and moved to the USA in my early 20s. My parents ran a printing shop when I was growing up in Seoul, and they brought all sorts of paper home. I was never short of paper, which made me very fortunate for someone growing up at that time. I was constantly drawing and making things out of paper. I discovered paper sculpture in my late 20s, and started developing my career as an independent artist and a freelancer. I have had a number of solo and group exhibitions and have worked on commissions for individuals, non-profit organizations and commercial clients. I also hold demonstrations at conferences and workshops. I run an online shop at *www.etsy.com/shop/papernoodle*. My artworks can be seen at *www.papernoodle.com* and *www.flickr.com/photos/papernoodle*.

# Acknowledgements

Writing this book has been an incredible journey. I used to wish I could make paper sculpture all the time, day and night, and I got to do that while working on this book. I had so much fun. People say that you learn more about something when you teach others, and that was true. I got to organize my thoughts and knowledge, and now I love paper sculpture even more. All these wonderful experiences could not have happened without endless sacrifices and support from my family. I have some serious making up for all the things they did for me, and I can't wait. I dedicate this book to my husband, my son, my mother-in-law and my father-in-law.

I also must mention how grateful I am to Jonathan Bailey, who gave me this wonderful opportunity, and all the editors who helped me go through my first book-writing experience.

# Index

Projects are in **bold**.

To place an order, or request a
catalogue, contact:

GMC Publications Ltd
Castle Place, 166 High Street,
Lewes, East Sussex, BN7 1XU
United Kingdom

Tel: +44 (0)1273 488005
Fax: +44 (0)1273 402866

www.gmcbooks.com